Public Economics in Action

The Basic Income/Flat Tax Proposal

A. B. Atkinson

D0171223

CLARENDON PRESS · OXFORD

HJ4629
.A8
1995
i 0198 283369

Oxford University Press, Walton Street, Oxford OX2 6DP
Oxford New York
Athens Auckland Bangkok Bogota Bombay
Buenos Aires Calcutta Cape Town Dar es Salaam
Delhi Florence Hong Kong Istanbul Karachi
Kuala Lumpur Madras Madrid Melbourne
Mexico City Nairobi Paris Singapore
Taipei Tokyo Toronto
and associated companies in
Berlin Ibadan

Oxford is a trade mark of Oxford University Press

Published in the United States by
Oxford University Press Inc., New York

© A. B. Atkinson, 1995

First published 1995
Reprinted in hardback 1996
First published in paperback 1996

All rights reserved. No part of this publication may be reproduced,
stored in a retrieval system, or transmitted, in any form or by any means,
without the prior permission in writing of Oxford University Press.
Within the UK, exceptions are allowed in respect of any fair dealing for the
purpose of research or private study, or criticism or review, as permitted
under the Copyright, Designs and Patents Act, 1988, or in the case of
reprographic reproduction in accordance with the terms of the licences
issued by the Copyright Licensing Agency. Enquiries concerning
reproduction outside these terms and in other countries should be
sent to the Rights Department, Oxford University Press,
at the address above

This book is sold subject to the condition that it shall not, by way
of trade or otherwise, be lent, re-sold, hired out or otherwise circulated
without the publisher's prior consent in any form of binding or cover
other than that in which it is published and without a similar condition
including this condition being imposed on the subsequent purchaser

British Library Cataloguing in Publication Data
Data available

Library of Congress Cataloging in Publication Data
Atkinson, A. B. (Anthony Barnes)
Public economics in action: the basic income / flat tax proposal /
A. B. Atkinson.
Includes bibliographical references and index.
1. Income tax.   2. Flat-rate income tax.   3. Social security—
Finance.   4. Guaranteed annual income.   5. Social choice.
I. Title.
HJ4629.A8 1995   336.24—dc20   94-36055
ISBN 0-19-828336-9
ISBN 0-19-829216-3 (Pbk)

Printed in Great Britain
on acid-free paper by
Biddles Ltd, Guildford and King's Lynn

Public Economics in Action

The Lindahl Lectures

Tax Reform and the Cost of Capital
Dale W. Jorgenson and Kun-Young Yun (1991)

Series Foreword

The Lindahl Lectures on Monetary and Fiscal Policy have been instituted by Uppsala University with support from Nordbanken as a biannual event to honor the memory of Erik Lindahl (1891–1960). Lindahl was a great economist who held a chair in economics at the University between 1942 and 1958. A concise but thorough account of Lindahl's scientific contributions with a selective bibliography has been published by Otto Steiger.[1] A more extensive account, including many valuable biographical details, has been presented by Jan Petersson.[2]

Lindahl's contributions fall mainly within four areas:
1. National income accounting.
2. Public finance.
3. Monetary and macroeconomic theory.
4. Stabilization policy.

National accounts are essential for the design of tax policy and stabilization policies. Lindahl developed a consistent intertemporal framework for the basic concept of income by relating it to capital, the pricing of capital goods, and capital gains and losses. He also devoted much time and effort to initiating the empirical measurement of national income movements over time in Sweden. His extremely meticulous work with social accounting concepts has proved to be of such lasting value that it led Sir John Hicks to call him 'the father of Social Accounting theory.'[3]

In public finance Lindahl greatly advanced Knut Wicksell's benefit approach to taxation. His theoretical model for distribut-

1. 'Erik Robert Lindahl,' in John Eatwell, Murray Milgate, and Peter Newman (eds.), *The New Palgrave*, New York, The Stockton Press, 1987, Vol. 3, pp. 194–198.
2. 'Erik Lindahl', in Ragnar Bentzel *et al.* 'Economics at Uppsala University. The Department and its Professors since 1741', *Acta Universitatis Upsaliensis. Studia Oeconomica Upsaliensia* 23, 1993, pp. 71–92.
3. John R. Hicks, 'Recollections and Documents,' *Economica*, Vol. 40, No. 157, February 1973, pp. 2–11.

ing the costs of public goods through a political analogue to markets for private goods is a standard reference in tax policy. He also did a substantial amount of empirical work, directed towards measuring the total tax burden and analyzing the effects of double taxation of saving through company taxation. He participated in an international comparison of the burden of taxation in different countries.

Best remembered and most highly regarded among Lindahl's contributions is his pioneering work in macroeconomics as a leader of the Stockholm School. In fact, the term 'macroeconomics' was first introduced into economic parlance by Lindahl. If Wicksell was the first to formulate the idea of 'disequilibrium dynamics,' Lindahl was one of the first, and perhaps the first, to develop this into a general area of research. He devised a novel methodology for economic dynamics and introduced many concepts that have become standard in economics, such as temporary equilibrium and the 'natural rate' of unemployment.

Like all Swedish economists of his time, Lindahl was intensely interested and involved in current economic problems and policies. He directed much of his work at finding solutions to the pressing problems of the inter-war years, namely, the stabilization of prices, output, and employment. To the Swedish public, he became best known for his fight against inflation after World War II, as an adviser to the *Riksbank*. According to Lindahl, a stable price level should be the declared aim of an independent Central Bank. This target should be reached by using the bank's control of the term structure of interest rates to influence the market's anticipations of future prices.

As Lindahl realized, monetary policy by itself is not sufficient to deal with unemployment problems during depressions. He proposed to complement monetary policy by compensatory fiscal policy, letting the budget balance vary inversely with the business cycle. As Ragnar Frisch stated in 1947, 'Lindahl . . . was one of the first, if not the first, to bring out the view that the essence of problems of public finance resides in the relations that link public finance to monetary policy, and to emphasize the role of the combined monetary and fiscal policy as tools of promoting full employment on a high level of real income and economic welfare.'

This describes perfectly why Uppsala University has thought it fitting to commemorate the work of Erik Lindahl by a series of lectures on monetary and fiscal policy.

Bengt-Christer Ysander
Uppsala   March 1991

Preface

This book contains a substantially revised version of the Lindahl Lectures given at the University of Uppsala in April 1989, and the background material on which they were based. I am most grateful to the Uppsala Department of Economics for their invitation to deliver the lectures and for their hospitality during my visit. My principal host in Uppsala was Bengt-Christer Ysander, and I much appreciated the warmth of the welcome he extended to me. It is a matter of deep sadness that he died on 23 March 1992; he is greatly missed by those who knew him and by the economics profession at large.

The Lectures aim to survey recent developments in public economics by taking as a case-study proposals for a basic income scheme. My research on public economics over the past twenty-five years has benefited particularly from collaboration with Joe Stiglitz, Nick Stern, Mervyn King, and François Bourguignon, and their influence on my thinking will be evident. The sections on the empirical aspects of taxation and social security draw heavily on the work of the Research Programme on Taxation, Incentives, and the Distribution of Income (TIDI). The Programme was located from 1980 at the London School of Economics in the Suntory Toyota International Centre for Economics and Related Disciplines (STICERD), which provided such a stimulating and helpful environment for research. I would like to express my appreciation to the Economic and Social Research Council (ESRC) for its support over a period of twelve years, and to all those who have been associated with the Programme. In particular, it is a pleasure to acknowledge the major contribution made by Holly Sutherland to the development of the TAXMOD model (the model is now POLIMOD and is available from the Microsimulation Unit which she directs in the Department of Applied Economics at Cambridge). TAXMOD makes use of material from the Family Expenditure Survey made available by the Central Statistical Office (CSO) through the ESRC Data Archive by permission of the Controller of HM Stationery Office. Neither the CSO nor the ESRC Data Archive bear any responsibility for the analysis or interpretation of the data reported here.

I was first prompted to look at basic income schemes by James Meade, who has contributed greatly to our understanding of their implications (for example, Meade 1948 and 1972). Not only did he regale me with stories about the early proponents of the idea, such as Lady Juliet Rhys-Williams (author of *Something to Look Forward to*, 1943), but he persuaded me to give a seminar in Cambridge on the topic in 1968, which led to my first book, *Poverty in Britain and the Reform of Social Security* (Atkinson 1969). He continued to encourage me to take the idea seriously, not least when I was a member of the Meade Committee on tax reform. He put me in touch with the late Sir Brandon Rhys Williams MP, who developed his mother's original ideas, most recently in association with Hermione Parker. Hermione spent a period in STICERD working on basic income schemes and I learned a lot from our exchanges and from her book, *Instead of the Dole* (Parker 1989).

The first draft of the lectures was written in the spring of 1989 at the European University Institute at Florence, and delivered as a course of lectures there. I am grateful to the Institute for its hospitality and for providing such an excellent working environment. In the course of writing the lectures, I also produced a number of papers, circulated first in the TIDI Discussion Papers series as Numbers 123 and 142 (with H. Sutherland), 135 and 136, and later published as Atkinson and Sutherland 1989 and 1990, and Atkinson 1990 and 1991*a*.

In preparing the lectures for publication, I have revised and rearranged the material, while trying to keep as close as possible to the original presentation. The eight chapters contain the substance of the lectures, together with an additional section on the general equilibrium incidence of taxes and benefits. With the interests of a student readership in mind, I have also added further details of the theoretical models and of the empirical calculations; this has made the book more technical, but I hope that none the less it succeeds in conveying the flavour of the original lectures.

A. B. A.

Cambridge,
February 1994

Contents

List of Figures

List of Tables

1   A First Look at the Issues

1.1 Introduction

The topic of these Lectures is, I hope, an appropriate one to honour Erik Lindahl, an economist whose contributions have been of lasting importance. In the area of his interests to which I shall be referring—public finance—the issues with which he was concerned are very much alive today. This applies particularly to the field of public choice theory, which to a considerable extent owes its origins to Scandinavian scholars such as Wicksell and Lindahl.

The aim of the Lectures is to take one particular problem of policy interest in the field of taxation and social security and use it as a basis for assessing the current state of public economics. That is, I would like to review some of the different areas in which there has been active research in recent years—notably the theory of optimum taxation, general equilibrium analysis of incidence, the theory of public choice, numerical tax-benefit modelling, and econometric studies of incentives—and to ask how these contribute to our understanding of one concrete policy reform. What can be said on the basis of current knowledge and what are the promising directions for future research?

The particular policy proposal that I take as a case-study would affect both personal income taxation and the social security system, replacing the one by a flat-rate income tax and the other by a guaranteed basic income. The proposal of a *basic income/flat tax*, or variations on its central elements, has generated wide interest in a number of countries. The idea is being actively discussed by a number of political groups. It is not my purpose to argue for or against the introduction of such a scheme, but it is certainly my view that it should be on the agenda for any serious discussion of tax and social security reform for the twenty-first century.

The structure of the Lectures when presented in Uppsala took account of the well-attested sociological fact that many people only attend the first of a series of three lectures. The first Lecture therefore was a *tour d'horizon*, covering the whole field in a preliminary way. The same is attempted here in Chapter 1, which is intended to introduce the reader to the material dealt with in subsequent chapters and to provide a rapid impression of the line of argument.

1.2 The Basic Income/Flat Tax Proposal

In essence, the scheme considered here consists of the payment of a basic income to everyone in the population (with possibly differing amounts according to age). This basic income would, in the pure form of the scheme, replace all social security benefits. The impact on those currently receiving such benefits would depend on the level of the basic income relative to existing social security. For those without such benefits at present, and with no taxable income (such as married women not in paid work), the basic income would represent a net gain. For those with taxable income, the new scheme would also replace all income tax allowances, so that income tax would become payable on all income from the first £1. The net gain would depend on the amount of the basic income relative to the value of the existing allowances.

The new tax would replace the existing income tax and social security contributions. It is proposed that the tax rate be the same on all income: there would be a flat tax. Although it would be quite possible to combine the basic income with a graduated rate schedule, the initial tax rate necessary to finance an adequate basic income is likely to be close to the present higher rate of tax in Britain (40 per cent in 1989), so that the scope for graduation would in practice be limited, and I concentrate in this chapter on the Basic Income/Flat Tax (BI/FT) package.

Support for such a reform comes from a wide variety of sources. It is undoubtedly the case that many of the supporters of a basic income are those who favour greater redistribution. There is much concern about those at the bottom of the income scale, particularly in the face of widening inequality in pre-tax incomes. One major argument is that the basic income would provide help to low-paid workers, who do not at present derive as much benefit as the better off from tax allowances. In effect the basic income scheme replaces a tax allowance (whose value rises with the marginal tax rate, and hence with income) by a refundable tax credit (the value of which is the same for all). It would help those not in work who do not qualify for social security benefits.

A second feature of the basic income which has been stressed is that it would be a totally independent system: all adults would receive a basic income regardless of marital status and of the circumstances of their partner. The flat income tax would be entirely independent: since all income is taxed at the same rate, there is no need to define a tax unit. As noted above, among those who would directly benefit are married women not in paid work, and in this respect the BI/FT scheme is seen as reducing gender inequities: 'Women do badly out of the existing social security system . . . Women would do better out of a Basic Income' (Parker 1993: 61). Men may also benefit from the independence of a basic income. For example, where they are unemployed but their partner is in employment, then they may at present not be eligible for social assistance, but they would receive the basic income in their own right.

A third aspect of the basic income which finds favour is that it would not depend on employment status. There would be no special payment to those who are unemployed, as under social insurance or social assistance. A person returning to work, whether part time or full time, would not lose benefit. The 'unemployment trap' would disappear. The basic income would do away with the need for tests of availability for work or of voluntary unemployment. This is welcomed, on the one hand, by those concerned that the stringency of the tests is such that a significant number of eligible claimants are incorrectly rejected, and, on the other hand, by those who suggest that the tests are too lax, so that there is a disincentive to return to work.

A fourth set of arguments centre on the reduction in administration costs for government and taxpayers. The basic income would do away with the present complicated means-tested benefits. The elimination of categorical tests for benefit receipt would offer administrative savings, as would the reduction in differentiation of benefit amounts. Individuals would no longer have to pay parallel taxes on income and contributions on earnings, thus avoiding duplicate assessments. The flat tax would be simpler to administer than the present graduated rate structure.

These considerations have provided the basis for a broad coalition of support for the basic income scheme. Proponents are to be found in all of the major political parties in the United Kingdom. Conservatives, or at least some of them, see the basic income as a quid pro quo for abolishing other forms of government intervention (such as minimum wage legislation), and they are naturally attracted by the flat tax idea. Socialists see the basic income as freeing people from dependence on the market economy, a position which has been shared by environmentalists; and some of them may regard a flat tax of, say 50 per cent, as a more effective redistributive device than a graduated rate structure. Liberals have long· advocated the integration of income taxation and social security.

The existence of such a 'rainbow coalition' of support for the Basic Income/Flat Tax idea does, however, raise questions. Can a single reform meet the very different objectives of different supporters? Would not freedom from dependence on the labour market be seen by conservatives as increasing dependence on the state? Would not the freeing of the labour market, welcomed by conservatives, be opposed by the left as weakening the power of the low paid? Would there not be disagreement about key aspects such as the rate of tax? In the British context, would there be 'levelling up' to a tax rate of 40 per cent or 'levelling down' to a rate of 25 per cent? What would be the economic and social implications of the wide-ranging reform that BI/FT would involve? Would there be an adverse impact on wage levels and other incomes? These questions are important since they may throw light on the reasons why the advocates of a basic income have so far failed to persuade governments to introduce such a scheme.

The aim of these Lectures is to examine what public economics can contribute to answering these questions. In recent years, public economics has developed in several important directions and we may identify at least five different types of research relevant to the examination of the BI/FT proposal:

(*a*) optimum income taxation,
(*b*) public choice,
(*c*) general equilibrium analysis of incidence,
(*d*) tax-benefit models,
(*e*) econometric studies of incentives.

In the course of the book, I consider in turn the contribution of each of these, and they form the subject of Chapters 2–7 (there are two chapters on optimum taxation). As already explained, in this first chapter, I cover all five in a preliminary way, although in a different order. I start with optimum taxation, leading into econometric evidence on incentives and the general equilibrium treatment of incidence, then going on to public choice theory, and ending with tax-benefit models.

1.3 Optimum Taxation

Lindahl opened his essay in the Festschrift for Bertil Ohlin with the observation that 'the study of the principles of taxation . . . seems in recent years to have fallen in disrepute' (1959: 7). Thirty years later, one could hardly write the same, since there has been in the meantime an explosion of literature on the welfare economics of taxation. One branch of this literature— that on optimum linear income taxation—is directly relevant to the BI/FT proposal, and it is with this that I begin.

The central issue considered in the analysis of the optimum linear tax is precisely that of choosing between different levels of the basic income guarantee, denoted by B, and the associated tax rate, t. In making this choice, the government is assumed to be constrained by a government budget balance requirement and by the responses of taxpayers. The latter are evidently important in introducing the supply side of the economy, which was a concern of public finance economists long before it became politically fashionable: for example, Lindahl in 1928 said that 'it is above all imperative to consider all the numerous side effects of taxation on the size of national income' (1928: 231).

In the optimum income tax literature, the supply side is introduced by the fact that taxpayers are assumed to adjust their labour supply in response to changes in taxation. This

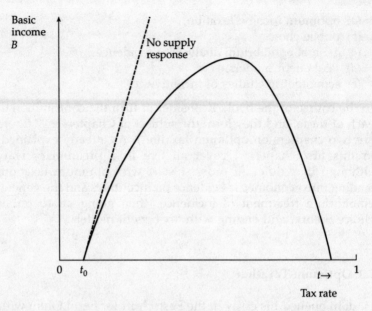

Fig. 1.1   Menu of possibilities for the basic income

may be illustrated graphically—see Figure 1.1. It is assumed that some minimum tax rate, t_0, is necessary to finance other items of expenditure; at this level the basic income, B is zero. If the government chooses a higher tax rate, then the revenue rises and B becomes positive. If there were no supply-side response, then B could rise linearly with t along the dashed line, but the typical supply response leads to a menu that is less favourable, with total labour supply, and hence total revenue, being reduced as the tax rate rises. Indeed, as Jules Dupuit pointed out in 1844, and Arthur Laffer has since reminded us, the curve may well reach a peak, and then decline.

   In order to be more concrete, let us suppose that everyone is identical and that labour is measured in terms of hours of work, L, and that these are supplied according to the constant elasticity function:

$$L = L_0 \, [w(1 - t)]^\varepsilon \tag{1.1}$$

so that ε is the elasticity of labour supply with respect to the net wage, w being the gross wage rate per hour and L_0 a constant. It may be noted that this labour supply function is unaffected by the receipt of any income from other sources (such as the basic income) and that, with ε positive, the labour supply function is upward-sloping. (ε is the compensated, or substitution, elasticity.) With this simple formulation, which I will use for illustrative purposes in much of the book, the revenue, and hence the basic income, increases with the tax rate until it reaches the value of $1/(1 + ε)$ and then declines to zero at $t = 1$. (In Figure 1.1, the curve for B hits the axis before $t = 1$ in view of the need for revenue for other purposes.)

A world in which everyone is identical, *ex post* as well as *ex ante*, would not, however, give rise to the problem of redistribution which is at the heart of the Basic Income proposal. This means that we must introduce an explanation as to why people differ. The difference on which attention has focused is that in earning power: in the wage rate, w, per hour. There are assumed to be no other sources of income. There are also assumed to be no differences in preferences, so that all people with the same wage rate supply the same amount of labour. This is evidently a highly stylized situation, and the model can only be regarded as a simple laboratory within which to explore the implications of different arguments.

Moreover, in calculating the formulae it is convenient to assume that the distribution of wage rates, w, is lognormal with a coefficient of variation, η. In other words, the logarithm of w is normally distributed. The degree of inequality increases with η: a value of 0.2 means that the upper quartile (person 25 per cent from the top) has a wage rate 30 per cent higher than that of the person at the lower quartile (25 per cent from the bottom), whereas a value of 0.4, which may be more relevant in Britain, means that the difference is 68 per cent. The difference in total earnings (i.e. $w \times L$) is greater with the labour supply function assumed here, since hours increase with w. With an elasticity of 0.5, for example, the upper quartile is 49 per cent higher in the former case and 117 per cent higher in the latter case. In Great Britain in April 1990, the upper quartile of total gross weekly earnings for all full-time employees (whose pay was not affected by absence) was 92 per cent higher than the lower quartile (Department of Employment 1990, Part A, Table 17).

These elements determine the menu of choice. What now are the kinds of arguments that would lead us to choose one point rather than another from the menu? The optimum taxation literature proceeds by assuming that our objectives are 'welfarist' in the sense that the social welfare function depends only on individual welfares and that these enter positively (or, at least, non-negatively). This is very much in the tradition of welfare economics, but is restrictive, as I argue later. A convenient, if over-simplified, way of representing such an objective function is to say that the social value of an additional unit of income (the *social marginal value of income*) to a person with wage rate w is proportional to

$$w^{-\gamma} \tag{1.2}$$

As it was put by Arthur Okun (1975), taking different values of γ allows us to represent different views about the desirability of redistribution, ranging from those of Milton Friedman to John Rawls. Friedman, he suggests, would set γ equal to zero, which would give *distributional indifference*, the social marginal value of income being the same for everyone. Whereas, according to Okun's interpretation of Rawls, we should apply the weights obtained by taking the appropriate limit as γ tends to infinity. In this case, all the weight is placed on the least advantaged. (I should stress that this interpretation does not adequately reflect the richness of the theory of justice of Rawls 1971, a point to which I return below.) Okun's own preference was for an intermediate case, which we can represent by taking a value of one half. This means that if a rich man has a wage nine times that of a poor man, then we only attach one-third of the weight to an increase of £1 in his income.

With this formulation of redistributional objectives, we may solve for the choice of tax rate (see Chapter 2 for the derivation). The choice may be summarized in terms of the optimum tax rate, t^*:

$$\frac{t^*}{1 - t^*} = \frac{1}{\varepsilon}[1 - (1 + \eta^2)^{-\gamma(1+\varepsilon)}] \tag{1.3}$$

$$\underset{\text{efficiency}}{} \quad \underset{\text{equity}}{}$$

This formula provides, as indicated, the decomposition into efficiency and equity elements which is so popular among economists. The efficiency element is related solely to the elasticity of labour supply: other things equal, the larger the elasticity the greater the distortion caused by taxation and the smaller the optimum value of t. This is the analogue of the Ramsey formula in the case of indirect taxation, which indicates that tax rates should be lower on goods that are elastically demanded.

The equity element is more complex. It depends in part on the extent of inequality in wage rates as measured by η. As we might expect, the greater the inequality, the smaller this term and the closer the bracket to unity. One immediate consequence is that if other areas of policy lead to a widening of wage differentials, then there should be a compensating rise in the rate of taxation. A good example is provided by the removal of minimum wage protection. If this causes wage inequality to rise, then this strengthens the case for redistributive taxation.

The equity element also depends on ε, which appears because the larger the elasticity, the more gross earnings rise with w, and hence the more effective is the income tax as a redistributive instrument. And it depends on the distributional values embodied in γ. A person only concerned with total income ($\gamma = 0$) attaches no weight to redistribution, and concludes that t^* should be 0. As γ rises above zero, the equity term (in square brackets) becomes positive. Taking a value of $\gamma = \frac{1}{2}$, as preferred by Okun, the coefficient of variation of wages to be 0.4, and the labour supply elasticity to be 0.3, then the equity term is 0.092 and the optimal tax rate 23 per cent. In the limit of the Rawlsian case, as γ tends to infinity, the tax rate chosen is that which maximizes the level of the basic income: i.e. the top of the curve shown in Figure 1.1. The equity term is then equal to 1, and the optimal tax rate is $1/(1 + \varepsilon)$. With an elasticity of 0.3, this gives a tax rate of 77 per cent.

1.4 Quantifying the Equity/Efficiency Trade-off

The formula (1.3) incorporates equity and efficiency considerations into the design of a BI/FT in a theoretical way. A number of recent contributions have sought to render the trade-off between them operational. In doing so, they have drawn on the second type of analysis on my list—that of econometric studies of labour supply and other responses. The role played by empirical evidence is of course clear in that ε is a matter about which we require evidence. Moreover, it is evident from the formula that the choice of tax rate is very sensitive to the value of ε. Taking a value of $\gamma = \frac{1}{2}$ and the coefficient of variation of wages to be 0.4, as before, then an elasticity of labour supply equal to 0.5 would imply an optimum tax rate of 17 per cent, whereas an elasticity of 0.1 would imply that the optimum was 44 per cent. There is clearly a big difference between these two figures.

The measurement of the labour supply elasticity has been a major part of the research programme of empirical public finance. The past twenty-five years have seen significant advances in the use of cross-section micro-data; we have seen innovations such as the negative income tax experiments; there have been important developments in econometric methodology, such as those of Heckman on sample selection and of Hausman on the estimation of labour supply subject to non-linear budget constraints. The resulting estimates have in turn influenced the discussion of policy, a good example being provided by the work of Browning and Johnson (1984) for the United States, whose results are used here to illustrate the approach.

Browning and Johnson take a range of labour supply estimates, and make a number of simplifying assumptions, to calculate the cost of redistribution via a BI/FT package to different quintile groups (fifths) of the US population. For the case Browning and Johnson describe as 'most plausible', the overall average (compensated) elasticity is 0.312, or around the middle of the range just considered, but it should be noted that the average varies from 0.513 for the lowest quintile group to 0.255 for the fourth quintile group. The results may be summarized in terms of the gains or losses of net equivalent income (rounded to the nearest dollar) by different quintile groups from a 1 percentage point increase in the flat tax rate, used to finance a basic income (Browning and Johnson 1984, Table 8): Bottom 20 per cent, +$47; Next 20 per cent, +$33. The other three quintile groups lose on average. If the redistribution were purely a matter of sharing out a fixed cake, then the sum of these losses would be $80. However, the increase in the tax distorts labour supply decisions and reduces total (equivalent) income. It is this loss that generates the equity/efficiency trade-off. According to the estimates of Browning and Johnson, the losses are: Middle 20 per cent, −$11; Next 20 per cent, −$72; Top 20 per cent, −$196; so that the total of losses is no less than three times the total of gains.

Browning and Johnson conclude that 'the marginal cost of less income inequality is surprisingly high even when labour supply elasticities are relatively low' (1984: 201). One way of putting this is that the weights given to different income groups would have to decline quite rapidly with income for this redistribution to be seen as desirable. For example, if the bottom quintile have a weight of unity, and the next quintile a weight of a half, then we would need a pattern of something like:

Quintile	Weight	Weighted gain/loss
Bottom	1	+47
Next	$\frac{1}{2}$	+16.5
Middle	$\frac{4}{11}$	−4
Next	$\frac{1}{3}$	−24
Top	$\frac{1}{7}$	−28

in order for the plus items to outweigh comfortably the negative ones. Since the average net income of the top 20 per cent is about seven times that of the bottom 20 per cent, these weights correspond approximately to a value of $\gamma = 1$, or about twice that which was Okun's preference.

These findings of Browning and Johnson have contributed to an air of doubt about the possibilities for redistribution. Becker, for example, cites their study as evidence of 'the sizable burden of income taxes in the United States' (1984: 341 n). More generally, there have been many people arguing that, not only is it very costly to push redistribution further, but also that the existing transfers have gone too far. The article by Lindbeck (1986) called 'Limits to the welfare state' is an example, where he cites the work of Browning and others. There is, one might say, a sense of 'redistribution pessimism', derived from such attempts to incorporate empirical evidence into the social welfare evaluation. Applied to the particular case-study with which I am concerned here, we may deduce that the introduction of a Basic Income/Flat Tax would not offer the prospect of more effective redistribution.

1.5 Is Redistribution Pessimism Justified? Empirical Evidence

There are several reasons, in my judgement, why we should not necessarily draw such pessimistic conclusions from the analysis so far. Beginning with the empirical evidence, I have no doubt that this research has made considerable progress, and that we know a great deal more than twenty years ago. At the same time, we are also much more aware of the limits to our knowledge and the grounds for caution in drawing firm conclusions.

First, there is the choice of labour supply as the focus of attention, when there are other important areas of decision-making which may be affected by taxation—to a greater or lesser degree. It may be the growth of the economy that is our primary concern—dynamic rather than static efficiency. In order to investigate this, we need to look at decisions such as those regarding investment, savings, or portfolio choice. These decisions require a more extensive economic analysis—a point to which I shall return.

Secondly, labour supply itself has many dimensions, and the empirical evidence has tended to concentrate on only certain of these. The evidence on which I drew above referred to the effect on hours of work, whereas we have also to consider the impact on participation where the effect may be different. One of the advantages claimed for the basic income is that it would not affect the incentive of the unemployed to return to work. Less tangible aspects such as effort, morale, or willingness to take responsibility are less easily studied, as are decisions about the acquisition of skills and training. We might expect the total response to be larger when other dimensions are taken into account, but it does not follow that the effect of, say, the Basic Income/Flat Tax on the other dimensions operates in the same way or even in the same direction.

Thirdly, there is the choice of empirical evidence. Empirical

analyses based on cross-section surveys, as well as experimental studies, tend to produce results for subgroups of the
population. The estimates of Hausman (1981), widely quoted
in public debate (and discussed further in Chapter 7 below),
exclude the self-employed, people aged under 25 or over 55,
farmers, single women without children, and the disabled.
These exclusions reduce the degree of heterogeneity in the
sample studied, but mean that the results cannot be extrapolated
to the whole population. The reactions of the self-employed,
for instance, are likely to be rather different from those of
employees. Single women may respond differently from both
married women and single men.

Fourthly, the results of individual studies are often not particularly robust, there being a wide confidence interval about
the point estimates typically quoted, and, while there may be
some degree of congruence in the results from different studies,
they exhibit a range of variation which is large as far as the
present application is concerned. Conventional standards of
significance are in this respect not terribly helpful. An estimated
value of ε of 0.3 with a standard error of 0.1 might appear
satisfactory, but it would generate a 95 per cent confidence
interval nearly as wide as the range taken in the numerical
example at the beginning of this section.

Finally, there are the problems of interpretation. It is the
essence of an experiment (i) that taxpayers should be confronted
with different tax and benefit parameters and (ii) that there is a
control group to take account of the effect of other variables.
The problem with much of the available evidence is that one of
these conditions is not satisfied. In time-series data, there are
changes in tax policy, but they tend to be confounded with
changes in other variables. In cross-section data within a single
taxing authority there is no genuinely exogenous variation in
tax rates; and if we compare people living in different states (as
in the United States) or different countries, there remains the
problem of controlling for the differences between these
populations.

In setting out this catalogue of reservations about existing
evidence on incentives (discussed further in Chapter 7), I am not
suggesting that the empirical findings are biased in one direction or another—there are factors working in both directions.

Rather, it is important that the limits to our knowledge be recognized and conveyed to those drawing policy conclusions.

1.6 The Theoretical Framework

Turning to the theoretical framework, I feel again that there are reasons which suggest that definite conclusions may be premature.

The underlying assumption of the analysis is that of an Arrow–Debreu competitive economy with perfect information on the part of individual agents and full market clearing. Writing on public economics, including my own, has been too dependent on these assumptions. This limits the range of policy issues which can be addressed. In the present context, for example, we need to compare the basic income scheme with the existing alternative of social insurance/social assistance. A key difference is that the existing social security provisions are tied to specific contingencies such as unemployment or sickness, and in order to make a comparison, we need a model in which such contingencies can arise. Sickness introduces uncertainty; we need to consider the economics of the insurance market, with the associated problems of adverse selection and moral hazard, which may mean that there are incomplete possibilities for insurance. Unemployment may appear in the optimum taxation framework outlined earlier, in the sense of people choosing to work zero hours, but an adequate treatment needs to take account of a wider range of factors. Even remaining within an equilibrium theory of unemployment, we need to allow for efficiency wages, segmentation of the labour market, and involuntary unemployment.

The introduction of these considerations is particularly relevant to the *incidence* of the policy reform. In the simple optimum taxation analysis it was assumed that the factor prices (and, implicitly, the product prices) are unchanged by the introduction of the Basic Income/Flat Tax. There is assumed to be an infinitely elastic demand for labour of each quality at the specified wage rate. In contrast, the models of general equilibrium tax incidence of the type developed by Harberger (1962) tend to make simpler assumptions about the distribution, but to allow for changes in factor and product prices. They too are of the Arrow–Debreu type, with unemployment only appearing if labour is in excess supply at a zero wage rate, and what is needed is to extend these models to bring in other explanations of unemployment. This is developed further in Chapter 5.

The choice of underlying economic model is important for the kind of policy conclusions that are drawn. Outside the comfortable world of an Arrow–Debreu economy, it is no longer necessarily the case that taxes and transfers are distortions—imposing costs on an otherwise efficient allocation. It is quite possible, when we allow for real-world phenomena like incomplete information and the absence of markets, that the payment of benefits, or the levying of taxes, may improve the allocation of resources. In such a situation, the sum of the losses may not exceed the sum of the gains. There may indeed be circumstances in which tax/transfer policy can make everyone better off—even viewed in terms of their own narrow economic interest. I am not arguing that they would apply to the particular BI/FT proposal, but that we should consider such reforms in a context which at least allows such possibilities to arise.

1.7 The Formulation of Objectives

The objectives of policy are assumed in the earlier analysis to be embodied in a social welfare function. In a sense, the approach is flexible in that it allows us to incorporate different sets of distributional weights. These range from the equal weights of distributional indifference, which would lead us to reject the further redistribution in the example given above (since the sum of the losses exceeds the sum of the gains), to the case where all weight is attached to the bottom 20 per cent, and no weight to the other groups, in which case the further redistribution would certainly be approved.

In γ we have parameterized different distributional judgements. But the formulation is also very restrictive in that it assumes that the objectives of policy can be *fully* represented by a social welfare function based solely on individual welfares. (It is also the case that it has been assumed that individual welfares depend only on the circumstances of that person; no account is taken of interdependences, as where the welfare of better-off people is affected by the existence of poverty. I do not consider here such interdependences, which are the basis for the literature on 'Pareto-optimal redistribution'—see Hochman and Rodgers 1969.)

In my view, it is important to extend the range of objectives to include *non-welfarist* goals: i.e. those which are not based solely on considerations of individual welfare, as conventionally understood. Of these, there are a wide variety and at this point, I give just one example—that concerned with liberty or freedom. As already noted, the representation of Rawls's theory of justice described earlier was incomplete in that it concentrated on the difference principle (weight on the least advantaged) to the exclusion of his prior principle of liberty. According to this liberty principle, 'each person is to have an equal right to the most extensive basic liberty compatible with a similar liberty for others' (Rawls 1971: 60). This principle comes *prior* to the concern with the least advantaged referred to earlier. Only when this liberty principle is satisfied can we, according to Rawls, follow the difference principle.

Concern with liberty as a social objective long pre-dates welfare economics. The issue is how to make concrete its application to practical policy problems, such as that taken here. Does introduction of concern for liberty strengthen or weaken the case for a basic income in place of current provisions? That the answer is far from clear is illustrated by the discussion by Lindbeck (1988) of the role in the evaluation of the welfare state of freedom of choice, which he interprets in terms of marginal tax rates. He argues that high marginal tax rates mean that 'The individual is largely "trapped" in a certain income bracket *by government policies*, with very little possibility of changing his economic situation by his own effort' (1988: 299). There is therefore a case against high marginal rates quite independent of any disincentive effects.

How does the liberty objective, on this interpretation, affect our attitude to the Basic Income/Flat Tax proposal? To the extent that the flat tax rate would involve a high tax rate for the whole population—as opposed to just higher rate taxpayers as at present—it would mean that more people are placed in a situation where there is limited possibility of improving their economic situation by their own actions. At the same time, we have to remember that the highest marginal tax rates, in Britain at least, are those faced by *low* income groups as a result of means-tested social assistance benefits—which generate the 'poverty trap'. In 1989 approaching half a million families faced marginal tax rates of 70 per cent or higher (Atkinson and Sutherland 1990), largely as a result of the Family Credit scheme (which has a withdrawal rate of 70 per cent). One of the contributions of the BI/FT proposal is that the poverty trap would be abolished—and hence the possibilities of low income families to improve their situation by their own efforts would be significantly enhanced. It is not clear therefore whether the introduction of considerations of liberty—interpreted this way—would weaken or strengthen the case for the Basic Income/Flat Tax.

The interpretation of liberty just given is only one of many, and it may well strike non-economists as unconventional. In Chapter 4, other interpretations are discussed.

1.8 Public Choice Theory

The purpose of the optimum tax literature—and more generally the welfare economic approach to public policy—is sometimes misunderstood. It does not assume that policy is formed by some benevolent dictator who reads the *Journal of Public Economics* in order to find out what to do. The purpose of the analysis is rather to illuminate the structure of arguments, explaining the relationship between instruments, constraints, and objectives. At the same time, one must recognize that the constraints include those of political decision-making. One of the contributions of the public choice school has been to stress the structure within which political decisions are made and the need for a normative study of the way in which policy is determined. As it is put by Frey, 'Fiscal decisions *are* political, and if there is any economic influence it must be analyzed within an explicit framework of politico-economic interdependence. . . . otherwise one may end up with the "optimal tax" proposals being completely distorted in the democratic process' (1976: 32).

One development in the public choice framework has been that by Buchanan and his colleagues of the idea of a 'fiscal constitution'. According to this theory, Wicksell's idea of voluntary participation is applied to the constitutional stage of choice, when the rules of policy formation are determined, at which stage people are to a considerable extent uncertain about the implications of different rules for their own interests. They may therefore be guided by the kind of considerations which underlie the justification given by Harsanyi (1953) for utilitarianism or the original position of Rawls (1971). Or, they may have non-welfarist concerns such as liberty.

This approach seems particularly appropriate in the case of the BI/FT proposal, since the position of Brennan and Buchanan is that 'the major tax reform process (say of the Carter-type in Canada, or the British Royal Commission) is perhaps more like an attempt at a genuinely "constitutional convention" than any other common aspect of political life' (1977: 257). (The Carter Commission was a major enquiry into the Canadian tax system in the 1960s.) Seen this way, the constitutional choice is that between, on the one hand, the Basic Income/Flat Tax structure and, on the other, the present structure of social insurance/ assistance and graduated income tax rates, which I will refer to as Social Insurance/Graduated Tax (SI/GT). We have then two levels of decision-making. There is the

constitutional choice: BI/FT vs. SI/GT

followed by the

political machinery: t and B, or parameters of SI/GT

i.e. the second stage of political machinery determines the rates of tax and benefit. This means that the choice at the constitutional stage has to be made taking account of the fact that the actual tax rates and benefit levels will be governed by the political process. This process may be direct democracy, and the median voter model has been popular in theoretical and empirical public choice studies. It may be representative democracy, where political representatives are elected to carry out government. Or it may be, as Buchanan has emphasized, that the power of the bureaucracy is such that the government should be modelled as a 'Leviathan' seeking to maximize its size.

In this way, it seems to me, one can bring together optimum taxation and public choice perspectives, and this will be further elaborated in Chapter 4. For the present, we may note that this kind of political consideration has also led to a degree of pessimism regarding the Basic Income/Flat Tax idea. For example, it has been argued that, on the Leviathan theory, the broader tax base may allow the government to expand the revenue collected beyond the socially desirable level. Or, with a median voter view, it has been suggested that people will vote for larger redistribution since the majority with below average incomes can force those above the mean to pay. On this basis, whatever the intrinsic desirability of the BI/FT, in that tax and benefit levels *could* be set to achieve a social improvement, it is feared that the political machinery is such that the actually enacted outcome would be worse than the present situation with SI/GT. The same fears are expressed, from a different direction, by those concerned that the actual basic incomes would be set at too *low* a level. The overt payment of a guaranteed income, as opposed to a less obvious tax allowance, may attract greater political hostility; or the basic income may offer less scope for pressure group lobbying than the more fragmented social insurance.

Whether such pessimism on public choice grounds is warranted depends on the extent to which we accept the analysis of the political consequences of the basic income. This in turn depends on the validity of the underlying models of political behaviour, and it is not clear that the present modelling of the political process is sufficiently advanced to provide a firm basis for the kind of conclusions indicated. In the case of the median voter explanation, for instance, there is the difficulty that, once we move to two or more dimensions, the assumptions required to ensure that there is a well-defined majority outcome appear extremely restrictive, and not likely to apply in the present case. Moreover, political behaviour reflects social and cultural factors which are likely to differ significantly between countries. Explanations developed for the United States, for example, may have limited relevance in Europe.

Dismissal of the BI/FT proposal on public choice grounds may therefore be premature; and there is undoubtedly room to develop this field of research, notably in building a bridge between public choice and normative theories.

1.9 Economic Arithmetic and Tax-Benefit Models

I referred earlier to 'redistribution pessimism' in relation to the efficiency/equity trade-off. Doubts about the feasibility of the Basic Income/Flat Tax scheme have also tended to emerge from more elementary arithmetic calculations. The simplicity of the scheme in its pure form is indeed such that one can readily calculate the gross cost of the basic incomes, and work out the necessary tax rate on the new extended tax base (without any tax allowances), taking account of the revenue required for other purposes.

Past 'back of the envelope' calculations of this kind have indicated that a basic income in the United Kingdom set at the level of the flat-rate social insurance benefits for a single person, with a couple getting twice this amount, would involve a tax rate of 50 per cent or more. Even allowing for the fact that we are replacing both income tax and social insurance contributions, such a tax rate appears high, particularly when we remember that it makes no allowance for possible disincentive effects reducing tax revenue. It has led many of the supporters of the idea of basic income to conclude that politically it is not feasible. One notices in fact that many people swing from initial enthusiasm about the idea to regarding it as hopelessly utopian once they have looked at the arithmetic.

There is, however, an alternative, more constructive response, which is to seek to devise more refined versions of the scheme. In particular, it appears more profitable to see the Basic Income/Flat Tax, not as a 'greenfield' project, but as a process of *reform* starting from the present situation. (Historically, there are good reasons why the greenfield approach came to the adopted, since—in Britain at least—the proposals

of Lady Rhys Williams and others were for post-war recon-
struction.) This approach has led in turn to proposals for a
partial basic income, particularly by Sir Brandon Rhys Williams
and Hermione Parker (see Parker 1989), which would go part—
but not all—of the way towards replacing current social insurance. The aim is to achieve a significant part of the objectives
of the full basic income, without involving such a high tax
rate.

One version of such a partial basic income in Britain could be
achieved by replacing the present income tax allowances by
refundable tax credits, which would provide the embryo of a
basic income. The amount involved would be relatively small,
but it represents a starting-point. If, moreover, the flat tax were
introduced by taking the higher of the two rates in the UK,
rather than the lower, that is levelling up to 40 per cent rather
than levelling down to 25 per cent, coupled with some broadening of the tax base, then this would finance raising the basic
income quite substantially above the value of the present tax
allowance. While still not enough to permit social security
benefits to be completely abolished, it would represent a sizeable step in that direction.

Such a partial basic income cannot, however, be analysed on
the basis of 'back of the envelope' calculations. Both the cost,
and the effectiveness, can only be assessed by examining the
impact on individual taxpayers. For example, the extent to
which the partial basic income would float families off dependence on means-tested benefits depends on the individual circumstances of the family. It is here that we come to the final
area of public economics research considered here (and the
subject of Chapter 6): the construction of numerical tax-benefit
models. Models based on representative samples of the population are now widely used in the analysis of tax and social
security systems, and they have played a central role in discussions of possible reforms. Although some of these models
now incorporate behavioural responses in terms of changes in
labour supply or other decisions, an important role is played
by models which are purely *arithmetical*.

In research at the London School of Economics, one such
arithmetical tax-benefit model has been developed, called

TAXMOD (now POLIMOD), and we have used this to examine the implications of a partial basic income (Atkinson and Sutherland 1989). The first stage of such calculations is to arrive at a revenue-neutral reform, by iterating on one of the parameters, such as the level of the basic income or the tax rate. The figure for total revenue is built up by TAXMOD from calculations of the effect of the reform on the net incomes of individual families. These latter can be used to examine the distributional impact. For example, one can derive the average gain or loss of different decile groups in the population. Is it the case that the basic income scheme would benefit those at the bottom of the income distribution? If the lowest decile group in the population are on average gainers, are there still some in this group who lose? In other words, what is the distribution of gains and losses *within* decile ranges?

The results obtained from tax-benefit models—like those presented in Chapter 6—will no doubt raise questions in the mind of the reader. Those anxious to ensure that the gains from redistribution are 'targeted' on families in real need may be concerned to increase the degree to which the net gain is tapered as one moves up the income scale. Can the same redistribution towards the lowest income groups be achieved with a lower tax rate (and less redistribution towards those close to the median)? From a different point of view, readers may be concerned that within the bottom income groups there are families which lose, despite a sizeable average net gain, and ask whether the partial basic scheme income could be modified to avoid such losses.

It is because of the questions that tend to arise—and the differences in concerns of different users—that we have emphasized in our research the development of user-friendly models. In our view, use of the models should not be confined to specialists. Here advances in micro-computing have been of great importance, providing the access to computers and the increase in computing power which is necessary. The program TAXMOD has been written to run on ordinary personal computers and hence to be accessible to academics, journalists, politicians, members of pressure groups, and others engaged in the policy debate. (The model was run live in the third of the Lectures.)

Conclusions

In this chapter, I have tried to show that the Basic Income/Flat Tax proposal raises a range of interesting questions and that there are a number of branches of public economics that are relevant to trying to answer these questions. The aim of the rest of the book is to develop these aspects in greater depth.

2   Optimum Flat Tax and Basic Income

2.1 Introduction

In this chapter, I elaborate on the optimum linear income tax, discussed in simplified form in Chapter 1, and examine the light which it can cast on the Basic Income/Flat Tax (BI/FT) proposal, particularly the choice between different levels of basic income and associated rates of tax. Given that we have introduced a BI/FT, what are the arguments which support different choices from the menu of possibilities? How are the choices affected by changes in economic and social circumstances, such as increased wage inequality or an increased burden of dependency? The question of the choice between the BI/FT and the present Social Insurance/Graduated Tax arrangements is postponed to Chapter 3.

It is important to emphasize that the purpose of this analysis is not to provide precise numerical answers to these questions. We are not seeking to show that the optimum tax rate is 25 per cent or that it is 50 per cent. The aim of the analysis is to explore the structure of arguments leading up to answers. We are interested in the relationship between specified goals, assumptions about how the economy operates, and policy recommendations. We want to investigate the validity and robustness of the cases advanced for particular policies. Can we identify differences in social objectives which lead to differences in conclusions? Are the answers sensitive to the way in which the menu of possibilities is conceived?

The framework for the analysis of the optimum linear income tax is described in Section 2.2. Since the derivation of general results is not easy, I also work for illustrative purposes with a special labour supply function—that used in Chapter 1—and this is set out in detail in Section 2.3. The results of the optimum tax analysis are introduced in Section 2.4 with an account of the Rawlsian case. The general case is treated in

Section 2.5, and the explicit solution for the special labour supply function is presented in Section 2.6.

2.2 Framework for the Analysis

The central problem considered in the optimum income tax literature is the choice of a tax schedule which both raises revenue for other purposes, such as the provision of public goods, and achieves the desired redistribution among different taxpayers. The latter objective only arises where people differ and the central assumption, made in Chapter 1, is that people differ in their earning power, denoted by a wage rate, w, per hour. There are assumed to be no other differences between people: they have the same preferences and endowment of time. There are no other sources of income apart from earnings (and the basic income).

The situation considered here goes beyond that of Chapter 1 in that there is assumed to be a proportion, μ, of the population with zero earning power (on grounds of ill-health or incapacity); this group is referred to as the 'sick and retired' and represents the dependent population discussed in debates about the future of the welfare state. For the remaining $(1 - \mu)$, the wage is bounded below by w_0, where this is strictly positive. The wage rate is assumed to be distributed according to the cumulative distribution function, $F(w)$, where this represents the proportion of the total population (including the sick and retired) with wage less than or equal to w. Thus, $F(w)$ indicates the rank of a potential worker in the population, the ranks running from μ to 1 as w increases. The associated density function is $f(w)$. By construction, the distribution satisfies the condition

$$\int_{w_0}^{\infty} f(w)dw = 1 - \mu \tag{2.1}$$

Those with positive wage rates choose their level of labour supply, denoted by L, and this depends on the wage rate and on the tax system. In designing the latter, the government has to take account of the labour supply reactions. It is possible that, for certain values of the tax parameters, people may choose not to work (setting $L = 0$).

The instruments at the disposal of the government are taken here to be the basic income, B, and a constant tax rate, t, levied on earnings, wL. It is not possible for the level of B to be varied with earnings capacity or labour market status. The tax rate cannot be varied over the range of incomes. The reasons for these restrictions are not always spelled out in the literature, a point to which I return in Chapter 3. For the present, it should simply be noted that it is not necessarily inconsistent to suppose that the government knows the relation between L and w, and observes wL, but is not able to vary B (or t) with w. The apparent inconsistency may be due to the different status of different types of information. The government's knowledge of the labour supply relation may be based on statistical evidence (for example, drawn from a sample survey) which, while valid for designing the tax structure, is not acceptable in the calculation of individual taxes. The inferred value of w for an individual taxpayer cannot be the basis for a tax assessment.

The objective function at this stage is assumed to depend on individual welfares. More specifically, it takes the following additive form, where $\Gamma\{\ \}$ is a non-decreasing, concave (or linear) transformation:

$$\mu\Gamma\{v[B]\} + \int_{w_0}^{\infty} \Gamma\{V[w(1 - t), B]\}f(w)dw \qquad (2.2)$$

In this expression, $v[B]$ denotes the welfare of the sick and retired (which depends only on B), and $V[\ ]$ is the indirect utility function of those in the potentially working population.

The objective is maximized subject to the revenue constraint. If an amount R of revenue per person in the total population has to be raised for other purposes, the budget constraint per person is

$$B = t\int_{w_0}^{\infty} wLf(w)dw - R \qquad (2.3)$$

2.3 Special Case of Iso-Elastic Labour Supply Function with No Income Effect

The combination of assumptions about labour supply and the distribution of wage rates generates a menu of possibilities like that shown earlier in Figure 1.1, and, as there, I take for purposes of illustration the special case of an iso-elastic labour supply function with a zero income effect: i.e.

$$L = L_0[w(1 - t)]^\varepsilon \tag{2.4}$$

so that ε is the elasticity of labour supply with respect to the net wage (L_0 is a constant). This means that the level of the basic income has no direct impact on labour supply. It also implies that all potential workers do in fact supply positive hours; even with a wage w_0 the value of L is strictly positive.

Substituting the labour supply function (2.4) into (2.3), we obtain as the revenue constraint:

$$B = t(1 - t)^\varepsilon E\{w^{1+\varepsilon}\}L_0 - R \tag{2.5}$$

where $E\{x\}$ denotes the average value of the variable x taken over the whole population (including the sick and retired, for whom w is zero). It is convenient to express the basic income, and the revenue requirement, relative to the average earnings in the absence of taxation and basic income of those in the working population, $L_0 E\{w^{1+\varepsilon}\}/(1 - \mu)$, where the division by $(1 - \mu)$ adjusts for the proportion who are not in the potential labour force:

$$b \equiv \frac{B}{[L_0 E\{w^{1+\varepsilon}\}/(1 - \mu)]}; \quad r \equiv \frac{R}{[L_0 E\{w^{1+\varepsilon}\}/(1 - \mu)]} \tag{2.6}$$

With these re-definitions, the revenue constraint becomes

$$b = (1 - \mu)t\underline{(1 - t)^\varepsilon} - r \tag{2.7}$$

If there were no labour supply response, then the underlined term would be equal to 1, and the affordable basic income would be simply equal to the tax rate times the proportion of the population at work minus the revenue required for other purposes. In terms of Figure 1.1, we have the dashed straight line. The modification introduced by the labour supply response is given by the underlined term on the right-hand side of

Table 2.1 Iso-elastic labour supply function: shortfall from fixed labour supply assumption and feasible basic income

	t = 20%		t = 30%		t = 40%		t = 50%	
	SF	BI	SF	BI	SF	BI	SF	BI
$\varepsilon = 0$	0	17.0	0	25.5	0	34.0	0	42.5
0.1	2.2	16.6	3.5	24.6	5.0	32.3	6.7	39.7
0.3	6.5	15.9	10.1	22.9	14.2	29.2	18.8	34.5
0.5	10.6	15.2	16.3	21.3	22.5	26.3	29.3	30.1
1.0	20.0	13.6	30.0	17.9	40.0	20.4	50.0	21.3

Note: SF denotes shortfall from fixed labour supply assumption; BI denotes basic income where $\mu = 0.15$ and $r = 0$.

equation (2.7). The figures in Table 2.1 indicate the extent to which the feasible value of $(b + r)$ falls short of the 'fixed labour supply' assumption for different values of ε. The loss reaches 10 per cent for an elasticity of 0.5 if the tax rate is 20 per cent, but at an elasticity of 0.3 if the tax rate is 30 per cent. What level of basic income can be financed? Suppose that the sick and retired make up 15 per cent of the population ($\mu = 0.15$), then with an elasticity of 0.3 a tax rate of 20 per cent finances a basic income of 16 per cent of average earnings (in the absence of taxation) if there is no other revenue requirement ($r = 0$). (From equation (2.7), we can see that b is reduced by 1 percentage point for each 1 percentage point increase in the value of r.) A tax of 40 per cent would finance a basic income of 29 per cent of average earnings in the absence of other revenue requirements, but this would fall to 20 per cent if the labour supply elasticity were 1.0.

This illustrative example is a special one. In order to provide a point of comparison, I have included in the Appendix to this chapter a second special case, that where earnings are a linear function of the wage rate and of lump sum income. This alternative example has the property, among other things, that some people may choose not to work.

2.4 The Optimum Linear Income Tax

The model described in the preceding section provides a simple laboratory within which we can investigate the optimum linear income tax. The formulation is evidently highly stylized, but it has the advantage of incorporating the possible disincentive effects which are missing from much discussion of the desirability of redistribution, as typified by the cake-sharing analogy which is the basis for many philosophical discussions of principles of justice. If total income is unaffected by taxation, or by the payment of transfers, then there is no reason on efficiency grounds to stop short of 100 per cent marginal tax rates. In such a world, if individuals differ only in their wage rates, and are identical in their welfare functions, then there are no differences in the policies advocated by a Rawlsian from those favoured by those espousing a utilitarian philosophy. Both sets of moral values—and indeed any intermediate objective function—indicate that welfares should be equalized.

The cake-sharing model is therefore of little interest in this context. It is the existence of a trade-off between equity and efficiency that allows us to identify the differences between different social objectives. The model considered here, even if grossly over-simplified, is sufficiently rich to allow this aspect to be explored.

To begin with, I consider the case where the government is concerned only with the welfare of the least advantaged, referred to, following common practice, as a 'Rawlsian' objective. At this point, we should note that the formulation (2.2) leaves open the question of the comparability of the welfare levels of those in work and of the dependent population. If we assume that the utility functions are identical, then the least advantaged are the sick and retired, and the aim of Rawlsian policy is to maximize the basic income.

In Chapter 1, we saw that, in the special case considered here, the level of the basic income is maximized where $t = 1/(1 + \varepsilon)$, and this may be verified from equation (2.7). The optimum tax rate varies from 91 per cent when ε equals 0.1, to 77 per cent when ε equals 0.3, to 50 per cent when ε equals 1, to 20 per cent when ε equals 4.0. The level of the optimum tax rate clearly depends sensitively on the labour supply elasticity. The level of the basic income may be calculated from equation (2.7). Where ε equals 0.3, the proportion of the population sick and retired is 15 per cent, and no revenue is required for other purposes, the basic income is 42 per cent of average earnings per worker in the absence of taxation. The effect of the BI/FT is to reduce the average net income (including B) of those in the working population to 64 per cent of the pre-tax level, so that the basic income is in fact 64 per cent of the actual average net income for workers. This is high by the standard of BI/FT proposals, but would be reduced to 50 per cent if there were a revenue requirement for other purposes of 10 per cent.

It may be noted that the optimum Rawlsian tax rate does not depend on the size of the working population. An increase in the number of people who are sick and retired reduces the value of the basic income; it does not affect the tax rate chosen. In the numerical example just given, if the proportion of the population sick and retired rises from 15 to 25 per cent, the basic income falls to 58 per cent of the actual average net income for workers. This is a rather striking conclusion in the light of debate about the consequences of an increased dependency ratio for the welfare state. It suggests a simple policy rule: the full burden of adjustment to increased dependency should be borne by the replacement rate (b), with the average tax per worker remaining unchanged.

This, however, is a good example of the need for care in drawing conclusions from the optimum tax literature. The conclusion does not carry over to other objective functions (see the next section), and it lacks generality, as we discover by considering the second example given in the Appendix. With the linear earnings function, the first-order condition obtained by differentiating the right-hand side of equation (A2.6) with respect to t can be rearranged to give the following quadratic equation for the tax rate (it may also be checked that the second-order condition is satisfied):

$$\delta(1 - \mu)t^2 - (1 - t)^2 - \delta r' = 0 \qquad (2.8)$$

The resulting level of the basic income is given by

$$b' = (1 - t)^2 \left(\frac{1}{\delta}\right) \qquad (2.9)$$

So that if r' (the revenue requirement expressed as a proportion of average pre-BI/FT earnings of the working population) is zero, we can solve equation (2.8) for $[t/(1 - t)]$ as the
square root of $1/[\delta(1 - \mu)]$: for example, with $\delta = 0.3$ and $\mu =$
0.15 the tax rate is 66 per cent and the basic income is 37.5 per
cent of average earnings per worker in the absence of taxation.
In this case, the BI/FT reduces the average net income of those
in the working population to 65 per cent of the pre-tax level, so
that the basic income is 58 per cent of the actual average
net income for workers. (This solution is consistent with all
potential workers having strictly positive hours where the ratio
of the lowest wage rate to the average is greater than 39 per
cent.)

It may be seen from equation (2.8) that the optimum tax rate
is an increasing function of μ, and hence from equation (2.9)
that the basic income is a declining function. If a greater proportion of the population is sick or retired, then part of the
adjustment falls on the basic income. On the other hand, in
contrast to the situation with the first example, not all of the
adjustment takes this form, and the tax rate rises.

This suggests the need for caution in drawing qualitative
conclusions from simplified models. It might seem from the
first special example that there is a simple rule—that an
increased burden on the welfare state should be absorbed by
economies within spending—but this conclusion is not robust
to a change in the specification of the labour supply function.

2.5 General Optimum Linear Income Tax

What can in fact be learned from the optimum tax results? If
simple rules are potentially misleading, can we hope for any
other form of insight? One of the main functions of this literature is to illustrate the implications of different distributional
judgements, and this is the subject of this and the next section.

The Rawlsian objective is extreme in the sense that it attaches
all weight to the least advantaged. If we return to the more
general objective function (2.2), and introduce a Lagrange
multiplier, λ, associated with the budget constraint (2.3), then

where no potential worker chooses zero labour supply the Lagrangian has the form

$$\mu\Gamma[v[B]] + \int_{w_0}^{\infty} \Gamma[V[w(1 - t), B]]f(w)dw - \lambda[B + R - t\int_{w_0}^{\infty} wLf(w)dw]$$

(2.10)

The first-order condition with respect to the choice of B is

$$E\{\Gamma' . \alpha\} + \lambda t \int_{w_0}^{\infty} w \frac{\partial L}{\partial B} f(w)dw = \lambda$$

(2.11)

where $E\{\Gamma' . \alpha\}$ denotes the average of the social marginal value of income taken over the whole population, α being the derivative of the indirect utility function (either v or $V[\ ]$) with respect to lump-sum income. The left-hand side as a whole measures the social valuation of an additional unit of income being paid to everyone, taking account of the consequential changes in government revenue. It allows for the possibility that a worker reduces his or her hours of work as a result of receiving an increase in lump-sum income (i.e. that $\partial L/\partial B$ is negative), and hence pays less income tax.

The total effect, normalized by dividing by λ, of an additional unit of income on a person with wage rate w is defined as the *net* social marginal valuation; (see Atkinson and Stiglitz 1980: 387 and 409):

$$\phi(w) \equiv \Gamma' . \alpha/\lambda + tw \frac{\partial L}{\partial B}$$

(2.12)

and there is a similar expression, without the income derivative, for the sick and retired. The optimum tax involves, from (2.11), setting the basic income such that on average $\phi(w)$ is equal to 1. The uniform payment to everyone should be increased up to the point where the marginal benefit of an extra £1 is on average equal to the marginal cost of £1 per person (remember that we have denominated ϕ in terms of government revenue).

The rest of the solution follows from the first-order condition with respect to the choice of t. In order to express this condition in an intuitive form, we need to make use of the following property of the indirect utility function:

$$\partial V/\partial t = -\alpha wL$$

(2.13)

in other words the cost of a marginal increase in the tax rate is equal to the private marginal value of income times the amount of earnings subject to tax, and of the Slutsky relationship

$$\partial L / \partial t = -wS - wL \frac{\partial L}{\partial B} \tag{2.14}$$

Where S denotes the substitution term (labour response to a change in the net wage rate when compensated to remain at the same level of utility) and this term is non-negative. Differentiating (2.10) with respect to t, and using (2.13) and (2.14), the first-order condition may be written (Dixit and Sandmo 1977):

$$E\{wL \cdot (1 - \phi)\} = \frac{t}{1 - t} E\{wL \cdot \varepsilon(w)\} \tag{2.15}$$

where in calculating $E\{\ \}$, the average taken over the whole population, it should be noted that $L = 0$ for the sick and retired. The term $\varepsilon(w)$ denotes the substitution elasticity $(w(1 - t)S/L)$ for a person with wage rate w.

On the left-hand side of equation (2.15) are those elements that depend on the form of the objective function. This may be seen most clearly in the case where there are no income effects, so that the variation of ϕ with w depends solely on $\Gamma' \cdot \alpha/\lambda$ (see equation 2.12). (Where there are no income effects, we can drop the qualifying word 'net'.) In the Rawlsian case, the social marginal value of income accruing to those in work is zero, so that the left-hand side is $E\{wL\}$, and we have the solution described earlier for the constant elasticity case. The constant elasticity is simply replaced by the average elasticity, weighted by wL. If the social marginal valuation of income is constant for everyone—the government is indifferent as to who receives an extra £1—then ϕ is constant. From condition (2.11), it is equal to unity. This in turn implies that the lefthand side of (2.15) is zero. In the case of distributional indifference, the government does not levy an income tax and raises any necessary revenue by a uniform poll tax.

In between distributional indifference and the Rawlsian objective are cases where the social valuation of income declines with w, so that it is first above its average value of 1,

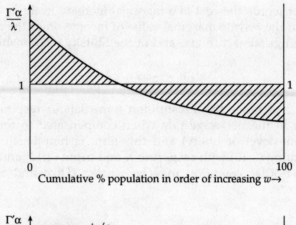

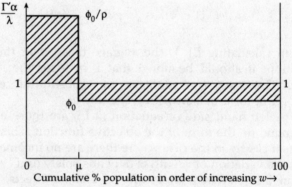

Fig. 2.1 Different distributional objectives and the social marginal value of income

and then below. The upper part of Figure 2.1 illustrates such a pattern, plotting the social marginal value at different percentile points of the distribution. The condition for the choice of B means that the shaded areas are equal. The left-hand side of (2.15) is formed by taking the difference from 1 and then multiplying by wL. If wL is an increasing function of w, then this gives more weight to the right-hand part of the distribution, where the social marginal value is less than 1, and hence makes the left-hand side of (2.15) positive. Put another way, the optimum tax rate depends on the covariance between wL and the social marginal valuation of income.

In general, the formulation (2.15) does not allow an explicit solution, and resort is made to numerical calculations, as in the work of Stern (1976). He takes a labour supply function that allows for different values of the elasticity of substitution between leisure and goods. In his central case, he takes a value for the elasticity of substitution of 0.4 and a revenue requirement of approximately 20 per cent of GNP. With a social welfare function such that the net social marginal valuation of income decreases as the square of income, the optimum tax rate is 54 per cent and the basic income is 34 per cent of the average income. He comments that 'The utilitarian approach therefore gives taxation rates which are rather high without any appeal to extreme social welfare functions, and need only invoke labour supply functions of the type which are commonly observed' (Stern 1976: 152).

2.6 Explicit Solution: Different Distributional Objectives

There are certain special cases where an explicit solution to the optimum linear income tax problem may be obtained, as with the iso-elastic labour supply function considered here. This means that the labour supply has a constant elasticity, so that we can take ε out of the integral on the right-hand side of equation (2.15).

The assumption about labour supply affects, however, not just the aggregate labour supply but also the distributional term. This latter effect operates through the weighting of $(1 - \phi)$ by wL on the left-hand side of equation (2.15), and through the evaluation of the welfare impact itself. The private marginal value of income, α, depends on the individual preferences underlying the supply of labour and on the way in which they are represented. For this, we have to go back to the indirect utility function, which in the case of the labour supply function with constant wage elasticity and zero income effect takes the form:

$$V[w(1 - t), B] = \left[\frac{L_0}{1 + \varepsilon}\right][w(1 - t)]^{1+\varepsilon} + B \qquad (2.16)$$

It may be checked that this yields the labour supply function (2.4), as does any increasing transformation of V. The particular cardinalization adopted in (2.16) is that which is the least concave representation, being linear in consumption (B). This provides a useful benchmark. It means that α is the same for all in the working population, and that any distributional preference is introduced via the social welfare function, Γ. (It may be noted that α is not the same for all in the benchmark case used by Stern (1976: 141), since the marginal valuation of an additional increase in income depends on w. This explains why he finds a positive optimum tax rate in this case.)

'Charitable Conservatism'

With this representation of the individual preferences, and in the absence of income effects, the social marginal valuation is given by $\phi(w) = \Gamma'/\lambda$ for those in work. How can we represent different distributional values? Suppose first that we consider the case of distributional concern limited to the dependent population, or what may be called 'charitable conservatism'. According to this set of values, there is a degree of concern for the dependent population, attributing to them a higher social marginal valuation of income, but this is the limit to the desired redistribution. On this view, society is indifferent with respect to the distribution among those in work: ϕ is constant ($= \phi_0$) for this group and lower by a proportion ρ (<1) than for those who are sick or retired. The value of the social marginal valuation of income is shown in the lower part of Figure 2.1.

What is the optimum BI/FT scheme in this charitable conservative case? The condition that the basic income be set such that, on average, the social marginal valuation of income is equal to 1 implies that

$$(1 - \mu)\phi_0 + \mu\phi_0\frac{1}{\rho} = 1 \qquad (2.17)$$

Returning to condition (2.15), we can see that the terms $E\{wL\}$ now cancel out, leaving $(1 - \phi_0)$ on the left-hand side. From equation (2.17), we can solve for ϕ_0 to obtain

Table 2.2 Iso-elastic labour supply function: optimum tax rate and basic income with different distributional objectives

	$\rho = 0.25$		$\rho = 0.5$		$\rho = 0.75$	
	t	*b*	*t*	*b*	*t*	*b*
Charitable conservative						
1.	50.8	34.9	30.3	23.1	13.7	11.2
Redistributive						
2. $\gamma = 0.5$	55.8	37.1	41.9	30.3	32.1	24.3
3. $\gamma = 1.0$	58.4	38.2	47.3	33.2	40.1	29.2
4. $\gamma = 2.0$	61.1	39.1	52.7	35.8	*	*
5. $\gamma = 3.0$	62.6	39.6	55.3	36.9	*	*
Rank order weights						
6.	62.6	39.6	55.3	36.9	*	*

Note: $\varepsilon = 0.3$, $\mu = 0.15$, $r = 0$ and Pareto distribution (for rows 2–6) with $\beta = 3$; * denotes condition (2.23) not satisfied.

$$\frac{t}{1-t} = \frac{1}{\varepsilon} \frac{1-\rho}{\left[1 + \rho\frac{(1-\mu)}{\mu}\right]} \qquad (2.18)$$

The parameter ρ is an indicator of the degree of concern for the dependent population, ranging from 1 (indifference) to 0, where society attaches no weight at all to the utility of the working population (the 'Rawlsian' case), and the right-hand side of equation (2.18) is simply $1/\varepsilon$. For values of ρ which are positive, but less than 1, the tax rate is less than in the Rawlsian case. The first row of Table 2.2 shows the optimal tax rate and the level of the basic income (calculated from (2.7)) for the situation where 15 per cent of the population are sick and retired and there is no revenue requirement ($r = 0$). Where ρ equals 0.75, in other words the dependent population get one-third additional weight, then a low level of tax and basic income is chosen, but where the dependent population get twice the weight of those in work ($\rho = 0.5$) the tax rate chosen is 30 per cent.

Redistributive Preferences

Suppose now that the distribution *within* the working population is a matter for concern, and that we have a 'redistributive' objective function. If social welfare is strictly a function of individual utilities, then $\Gamma'(w)$ depends on $V[w]$, and hence on the level of basic income and the tax rate. This dependence complicates the analysis; and in order to obtain an explicit solution I assume that the social marginal valuation depends only on w, and not on the level of utility. This assumption may be described as 'non-welfarist', but is implicit in a number of approaches to measuring inequality.

The first version of such a redistributive objective considered here is that adopted in Chapter 1, normalized so that the average weight for the working population remains equal to ϕ_0:

$$\phi(w) = \phi_0(1 - \mu)\frac{w^{-\gamma}}{E\{w^{-\gamma}\}} \tag{2.19}$$

The parameter γ measures the rate at which the social marginal valuation of income declines with the wage rate.

What is the optimum BI/FT with this set of social values? From (2.15), using (2.17), we arrive at the condition

$$\varepsilon\frac{t}{1 - t} = 1 - \frac{1}{[1 - \mu + \mu/\rho]} \cdot \frac{E\{w^{1+\varepsilon-\gamma}\}E\{w^0\}}{E\{w^{1+\varepsilon}\}E\{w^{-\gamma}\}} \tag{2.20}$$

The difference from (2.18) lies in the $E\{\ \}$ terms; if they cancelled (as where there is no inequality in wage rates), then we should have the same tax rate as with the charitable conservative position. Where there is inequality in wage rates, the redistributive preferences implied by a positive value of γ mean that the second term on the right-hand side is smaller, and hence that the optimum tax is larger.

In order to calculate the optimum tax in this case, we need information about the distribution of wage rates. Suppose that the distribution has the Pareto form with exponent β:

$$1 - F(w) = (1 - \mu)[w/w_0]^{-\beta} \tag{2.21}$$

which has the property that

$$E\{w^j\} = (1 - \mu)[\beta/(\beta - j)]w_0{}^j \tag{2.22}$$

From (2.19), we can see that the social marginal valuation of income for a person with the lowest wage rate is equal to $(1 + \beta/\gamma)\phi_0$. It seems reasonable to suppose that this is no greater than the social marginal valuation of income received by the dependent population

$$\left(1 + \frac{\beta}{\gamma}\right)\phi_0 < \frac{1}{\rho} \tag{2.23}$$

With an exponent of $\beta = 3.0$, the weight on the lowest-paid worker is twice the average where γ is equal to 3.0.

The values of the optimum tax rate, and of the basic income, in the case of a Pareto distribution may be calculated from the formula:

$$\varepsilon\frac{t}{1 - t} = 1 - \frac{1}{[1 - \mu + \mu/\rho]} \cdot \left[\frac{1 - \dfrac{1 + \varepsilon}{\beta}}{1 - \dfrac{1 + \varepsilon}{\beta + \gamma}}\right] \tag{2.24}$$

The results with $\beta = 3.0$ are shown in lines 2–5 of Table 2.2 for different values of γ and ρ. With γ equal to $\frac{1}{2}$, a value close to that preferred by Okun (1975), the tax rate rises to more than 30 per cent even where the additional weight given to the dependent population is only one-third (where $\rho = 0.75$). A person may support a tax rate of around 30 per cent, and a basic income of around a quarter, *either* through adopting the charitable conservative position and giving a double weight to the sick and retired (line 1 with $\rho = 0.5$) *or* because they give less weight to the dependent population ($\rho = 0.75$) but are concerned about redistribution within the working population.

Rank Order Weights

The second example of differential weights for the working population is that where the social marginal valuation declines according to the ranking in the wage distribution, again normalized so that the average over the working population is equal to ϕ_0:

$$\phi = \frac{2\phi_0(1 - F(w))}{1 - \mu} \tag{2.25}$$

For the working population this declines linearly with $F(w)$ from twice the average for the lowest-paid worker to zero as w tends to infinity. This is in effect the weighting underlying the Gini coefficient, as described by Sen (1974), who provided an axiomatic justification for such a social welfare function.

In the context examined here, the BI/FT does not change the rankings of individual taxpayers: it brings them closer together but does not reverse positions. The weights Γ' do not therefore depend on the tax parameters. In this case, Deaton (1983) shows that an explicit solution may be given for the linear earnings function described in the Appendix to this chapter. For the iso-elastic labour supply function used in this section, and the Pareto distribution of wage rates with exponent β, the optimum tax rate may be calculated to be

$$\varepsilon \frac{t}{1 - t} = 1 - \frac{1}{[1 - \mu + \mu/\rho]} \cdot \left[\frac{1 - \dfrac{1 + \varepsilon}{\beta}}{1 - \dfrac{1 + \varepsilon}{2\beta}} \right] \tag{2.26}$$

This coincides with that described earlier where $\gamma = \beta$—see the last row of Table 2.2, which shows the results where the weights on the dependent population are at least twice the average for the working population. It is interesting to note that the weights implied by the Gini coefficient correspond in this case to a relatively high value of the equity parameter.

2.7 Explicit Solution: The Equity/Efficiency Trade-off

According to many public finance texts, the central issue in the design of fiscal policy is the trade-off between equity and efficiency: for example, 'the trade-off between equity and efficiency is at the heart of many discussions of public policy'

(Stiglitz 1988: 91) and it was embodied in the title of the book by Okun (1975) cited in Chapter 1. But what exactly does this trade-off mean?

In the present model, a precise answer, or answers, can be given. The imposition of the income tax reduces the supply of labour and hence total earnings. In public debate, it sometimes appears that it is this reduction in total income which is identified as the 'efficiency cost'. There is a trade-off between GNP and inequality. Any reduction in output is regarded as a dead loss; and any benefit from the basic income is disregarded. In this case, with the iso-elastic labour supply function, we have to record that total income is reduced by a factor $(1 - t)^\varepsilon$.

In contrast, the welfare economic approach measures the efficiency loss in terms of the *reduction in utility*. In general, this will differ from the total income calculation in taking account only of the distortionary change in labour supply, that associated with the substitution effect, although in the present simple example there is no difference. It also differs in taking account of the basic income. From the form of the indirect utility function taken here (2.16), we can calculate, making use of the budget constraint, that where no revenue is required for other purposes, the average level of utility is given by $(1 - t)^\varepsilon(1 + \varepsilon t)$ times its no tax value. (This adds up utility with no distributional weights.) The fall is less than that in total income, on account of the second term. With a labour supply elasticity of 0.3, the reduction is modest, being only 4 per cent for a tax rate of 40 per cent. If the elasticity were 1.0, however, the reduction is by a factor of $(1 - t^2)$, which means a reduction of 16 per cent where $t = 40$ per cent.

How can this efficiency loss be put in the balance with the equity gain? Two broad approaches may be discerned in public and professional discussion. The first views *efficiency* and *equity* as two independent, fundamental objectives. The former may, for example, be seen as concern with making the best use of scarce resources; the latter may be egalitarian in origin or a weaker preference for distributional fairness. This position is stated clearly by Barry in his *Political Argument*, where he starts from the position that there are 'two very general principles which we may call "equity" and "efficiency" [and] for each person who evaluates in terms of these principles we can draw up a set of indifference curves showing along each line different combinations of the two between which he would be indifferent' (1965: 5). This approach belongs to a more eclectic and pluralist tradition. In contrast, the second approach sees efficiency and equity as means of achieving a maximum of social welfare; they are intermediate goals towards a more fundamental purpose.

It is the second approach which is followed in the optimum taxation literature, where efficiency and equity are essentially a way of interpreting the conditions for the choice of the optimum tax rate. Such an interpretation was given in Chapter 1, and I conclude the present discussion with a model identical to that used there, based on the redistributive weights (2.19) with the parameter γ. To this end, I simplify by assuming away the existence of the dependent population, setting $\mu = 0$, which means that $\phi_0 = 1$; and replace the assumption of a Pareto distribution by the—possibly more realistic—form of the lognormal (i.e. $\log_e w$ is normally distributed with mean m and variance v). We can then make use of the facts that

$$\log_e E\{w^j\} = jm + \tfrac{1}{2}j^2v^2 \qquad (2.27)$$

and that the coefficient of variation, η, satisfies

$$\log_e(1 + \eta^2) = v^2 \qquad (2.28)$$

Employing these formulae, we can obtain equation (1.3) of Chapter 1:

$$\frac{t}{1-t} = (1/\varepsilon)[1 - (1 + \eta^2)^{-\gamma(1+\varepsilon)}] \qquad (2.29)$$

The term in square brackets in equation (2.29) has been interpreted as the equity term, and $(1/\varepsilon)$ as the efficiency term. The interplay between these two elements is illustrated in Figure 2.2. On the horizontal axis is measured the degree of redistributive concern, where I have taken $\gamma/(1 + \gamma)$ in order to allow the full range within the unit interval. In the case of distributional indifference, we are at 0 at the left-hand side, and as ε approaches infinity (the Rawlsian position) we are at 1 at the right-hand side. The 'Okun' value of $\gamma = \tfrac{1}{2}$ is to be found at $\tfrac{1}{3}$ on the horizontal axis, and $\gamma = 1$ is at the halfway point. On the vertical axis is measured $1/(1 + \varepsilon)$, taken as an indicator

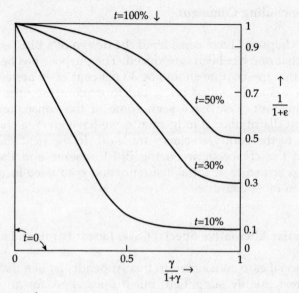

Fig. 2.2 Role of efficiency and equity considerations in influencing optimum tax rate

of the efficiency cost. As the elasticity tends to infinity, we have the maximum loss, and this is the bottom point of 0. As the elasticity becomes smaller, then we move upwards, approaching 1 as the elasticity tends to zero.

The value $1/(1 + \varepsilon)$ is that taken by the optimum tax rate in the Rawlsian case, so that the right-hand axis calibrates the choice of tax rate for the Rawlsian limit of distributional concern. We can plot iso-t contours, where the same value of t may be chosen by people with less redistributive objectives (smaller γ) but who consider ε to be smaller. These contours are illustrated in Figure 2.2 for the cases of $t = 10$ per cent, 30 per cent, and 50 per cent. A tax rate of 50 per cent, for example, may be chosen by a Rawlsian who believes that the labour supply elasticity is 1.0, or by a person less concerned with redistribution ($\gamma = 1$) but who believes that the labour supply elasticity is only 0.15. In the limit, a zero tax rate is chosen either by a person who is indifferent to the distribution (the left-hand vertical axis) or by a person who believes that the labour supply elasticity is infinite (bottom horizontal axis).

2.7 Concluding Comment

In this chapter, I have considered the design of a BI/FT scheme, given that one has been introduced. The purpose has been, not to say that the tax rate should be 30 per cent or 40 per cent, nor to derive simple policy rules, but to explore the structure of the arguments. We have seen some of the consequences of different distributional judgements; we have given a characterization of the equity/efficiency trade-off. In the next chapter, I turn to the choice between the BI/FT scheme and the more complex structure of social insurance and graduated income tax found in most countries.

Appendix: Alternative Special Case: Linear Earnings Function

The special case considered in this Appendix is, like that in the main text, highly simplified, but it does allow for an income effect on labour supply:

$$L = L^* - \frac{\delta B}{w(1 - t)} \tag{A2.1}$$

where $0 \leq \delta < 1$. This function is a version of that used by Deaton (1983) to obtain an explicit solution of the optimum linear income tax (see also Tuomala 1990: 77), and has the property that gross earnings are a linear function of the wage rate and lump-sum income. With the linear income tax, this means that net income

$$w(1 - t)L + B = w(1 - t)L^* + (1 - \delta)B \tag{A2.2}$$

It may be noted that this labour supply function is the same as the Cobb–Douglas form where $L^* = (1 - \delta)$; this form was used in the original article by Mirrlees (1971) and in Atkinson (1972).

An increase in the basic income reduces labour supply, as recipients 'spend' part of their additional income on increased leisure. The extent of the reduction is measured by the parameter δ, which represents the fraction by which net of tax earnings are reduced for a marginal increase in the basic income (or any other lump sum income). So that δ equal to 0.3

means that £10 increase in the basic income would lead to a £3 reduction in net earnings. The parameter also measures the responsiveness of labour supply to the net wage rate. The total elasticity of L with respect to $w(1 - t)$ is equal to δ times the ratio of B to $w(1 - t)L$. So that, with a basic income equal to a third of earnings (net of the marginal tax rate), the value of δ equal to 0.3 just taken for illustration implies a total labour supply elasticity of 0.1. As is noted by Deaton, to have 'a single quantity summarizing all disincentive effects is extremely convenient. It is also the single most restrictive assumption required to derive the results' (1983: 336).

A further difference from Special Case 1 is that, with the labour supply function (A2.1), some people may choose to live off the basic income and not to work. If the wage rate is below a critical value

$$w_- \equiv \frac{\delta B}{L^*(1 - t)} \tag{A2.3}$$

then the labour supply falls to zero. For the present, it is assumed that w_- is below w_0, so that everyone in the potential labour force is in fact working positive hours.

Substituting the labour supply function (A2.1) into the revenue constraint (2.3), we obtain

$$B = tE\{w\}L^* - \delta(1 - \mu)B\frac{t}{1 - t} - R \tag{A2.4}$$

It is again convenient to express the basic income, and the revenue requirement, relative to the average earnings in the absence of taxation and basic income of those in the working population:

$$b' = \frac{B}{[L^*E\{w\}/(1 - \mu)]}, \quad \text{and} \quad r' = \frac{R}{[L^*E\{w\}/(1 - \mu)]} \tag{A2.5}$$

This means that the revenue constraint becomes, after rearrangement

$$b' = \frac{t(1 - \mu) - r'}{1 + \delta(1 - \mu)t/(1 - t)} \tag{A2.6}$$

The modification introduced by the labour supply responses,

as B rises above 0, is given by the underlined term on the right-hand side of equation (A2.6).

The parameter δ plays, with this specification, the key role in summarizing the disincentive effects and hence the extent to which the feasible transfer falls short of that possible with a fixed cake. Suppose, as in the text, that the sick and retired make up 15 per cent of the population ($\mu = 0.15$), then taking a value for δ of 0.3, we see that a tax rate of 20 per cent finances a value of b' of 16 per cent if there is no other revenue requirement ($r' = 0$), and that a tax of 40 per cent would finance a basic income of 29.1 per cent of average earnings. These figures are similar to those with ε equals 0.3 in the previous example.

These calculations are made on the basis that labour supply is strictly positive for all of the potential working population, which requires in this case

$$b' < \frac{1-t}{\delta} \cdot \frac{w_0}{[E\{w\}/(1-\mu)]} \qquad \text{(A2.7)}$$

With the values of the parameters just used, and a tax rate of 40 per cent, this is satisfied where the lowest wage rate is greater than 14.6 per cent of the average for the potential working population. The constraint is in this case only likely to bind if there is a great degree of inequality in wage rates.

3 Optimum Taxation, Differentiation, and Graduation

3.1 Introduction

This chapter elaborates on certain aspects of the optimum income tax and the design of benefits. In Chapter 2, we examined the Basic Income/Flat Tax (BI/FT) proposal, looking at the choice between different levels of basic income and associated rates of tax, given that such a scheme was in force. The next important question concerns the choice between the BI/FT and the Social Insurance/Graduated Tax (SI/GT) arrangements found in most OECD countries. Here we need to consider both the graduation involved in most current income tax structures and the categorical nature of existing social insurance benefits, where a person qualifies by being unemployed, sick, etc. What considerations may lead us to be willing to abandon graduated taxes, with increasing marginal rates of taxation on higher incomes? What are the arguments for replacing existing categorical benefits by a universal basic income?

Historically, the question involves moving from the SI/GT structure to the simplified BI/FT scheme, but analytically the effect may be most easily seen by starting with the BI/FT scheme and asking whether we would like to depart from this by introducing graduated marginal rates and categorical benefits. This is the approach adopted here. Sections 3.2–3.4 are concerned with the case for graduation; Section 3.5 deals with categorical benefits. In neither case is the analysis more than suggestive. A full discussion of just the theoretical merits of the two systems would require substantially more space; to examine the detailed institutional issues is far outside the present scope.

3.2 Graduated Tax Rates

In most countries, the income tax structure does not have a single marginal rate of tax but involves a succession of rate bands with higher rates on higher tranches of income. In the United Kingdom in 1994 the personal income tax has a band at 20 per cent, followed by a long band at 25 per cent, and then a higher rate of 40 per cent. Ten years earlier, there had been a long band at 30 per cent, followed by rates of 40 per cent, 45 per cent, 50 per cent, 55 per cent, and 60 per cent. Moreover, in both cases the tax exemption takes the form of an allowance against taxable income, not a refundable tax credit, so that there is an initial band with a zero tax rate.

As a result, the individual taxpayer faces a non-linear budget constraint like that shown by $OABC$ in Figure 3.1. The net marginal wage is initially w until gross income reaches the tax threshold, Y_1, at the point A; the net marginal wage falls to $w(1 - t_1)$ when the person becomes subject to income tax at the initial rate; and then becomes $w(1 - t_2)$ in the higher rate band (where $t_2 > t_1$), which starts at B, where gross income is Y_2.

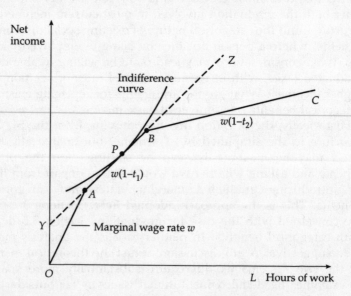

Fig. 3.1   Income tax with exemption and two tax bands

If the person has preferences between leisure and net income as shown by the indifference curve, the chosen hours of work are at P. This is the same choice as would be made if the person were confronted with the budget constraint $YABZ$: i.e. a constant marginal rate of tax t_1 and a basic income equal to OY. (The income OY is sometimes referred to as the 'virtual income'.) On the other hand, the person cannot choose from the dashed parts of this budget line. If, for example, he or she were to choose hours of work such that took them past B, then the higher marginal tax rate would apply.

What we have to do, therefore, is to piece together the labour supply function from what we know about the behaviour when faced with a linear budget constraint. For this purpose, I use here, and for much of the rest of this chapter, the iso-elastic labour supply function with no income effects which was the mainstay of the analysis of the previous chapter:

$$L = L_0[w_n]^\varepsilon \tag{3.1}$$

where w_n denotes the net of tax wage rate. The absence of an income effect means that L depends only on the slope, and not the intercept, of the budget constraint.

Considering different gross wage rates from zero upwards, there is an initial range where

$$L = L_0 w^\varepsilon \tag{3.2}$$

and this applies where gross earnings are below the tax threshold, or

$$w \leqslant w_1 \equiv \left[\frac{Y_1}{L_0}\right]^{\frac{1}{1+\varepsilon}} \tag{3.3}$$

There then follows a range of w such that a person chooses to stay at the kink A of the budget constraint. For w between w_1 and

$$w_2 \equiv \frac{w_1}{(1-t_1)^{\frac{\varepsilon}{1+\varepsilon}}} \tag{3.4}$$

the person would like to work more hours at a marginal wage w, but cannot, and would like to work fewer hours at a marginal wage $w(1 - t_1)$, but cannot. In this range, L is adjusted so that gross earnings are kept at the tax threshold:

$$L = \frac{Y_1}{w} \tag{3.5}$$

In other words, L is now a *declining* function of the wage rate—see Figure 3.2. At wages above w_2, hours of work increase according to the labour supply function with $w_n = w(1 - t_1)$, until the kink B is reached. There is then a range such that $L = Y_2/w$; this applies for wage rates between w_3 to w_4, where these are defined as follows:

$$w_3^{1+\varepsilon} = \frac{Y_2}{L_0(1 - t_1)^{\varepsilon'}}; \quad \text{and} \quad w_4 = w_3 \left[\frac{1 - t_1}{1 - t_2}\right]^{\frac{\varepsilon}{1+\varepsilon}} \tag{3.6}$$

Finally, for w above w_4, the choice of hours is that indicated by (3.1) with $w_n = w(1 - t_2)$. It is evident that even this—relatively simple—tax system generates a labour supply function which

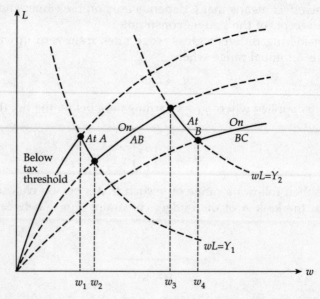

Fig. 3.2 Effect of graduated tax structure with exemption and two tax bands

is quite complex. This in turn has implications for the empirical study of labour supply, as discussed in Chapter 7.

In what circumstances would we prefer such a graduated rate structure, with increasing marginal rates of 0, t_1, t_2, to the simplified BI/FT? At first sight, it might appear that the addition of a further instrument must raise social welfare, or at least not lower it. There may be administrative or other considerations which mean that multiple rates are not desirable, but if we stay within the optimum tax framework the additional flexibility cannot reduce social welfare. It does not, however, follow that the optimum solution involves *increasing* marginal rates.

As has been shown by Slemrod *et al.* (1994), the optimum two-bracket income tax may involve a *lower* marginal rate on the higher bracket. Slemrod *et al.* perform numerical calculations similar to those of Stern (1976) quoted in Chapter 2. With a value of the elasticity of substitution between leisure and goods of 0.4, a revenue requirement of approximately 20 per cent of GNP, and a social welfare function that gives rather more weight to redistribution (the social marginal value of lump sum income declines as the cube of income), the optimal two-rate tax has rates of 60 per cent and then 52 per cent for the top 23 per cent of taxpayers, compared to an optimal single-rate tax of 58 per cent. There is a 'subsidy' to higher earnings to encourage them to work harder and generate more tax revenue. (For discussion of a wider range of issues affecting the choice between a dual rate or flat rate structure, see Kesselman 1990.)

3.3 Choice of Tax Structure

This brings us to the general question as to the appropriate shape of the income tax schedule, which was the original problem posed by Mirrlees (1971).

Suppose now that the government chooses a general tax function $T(wL)$, where T may be negative and in particular $-T(0)$ corresponds to the basic income received by those with no earnings. The government's choice is subject to the revenue constraint

$$B = \int_{w_0}^{\infty} T(wL)f(w)dw - R \tag{3.7}$$

The objective is to maximize the social welfare function

$$\int_{w_0}^{\infty} \Gamma\{U[L,X]\}f(w)dw \tag{3.8}$$

where for simplicity I have supposed that there are no sick and retired. The argument in the social welfare function is the level of utility as a function of labour and net income, X. For the iso-elastic labour supply function, the direct utility function may be written as

$$U(L, X) = X - \frac{(L/L_0)^{1+1/\varepsilon}L_0}{1 + (1/\varepsilon)} \tag{3.9}$$

where I have taken the least concave representation of preferences such that the private marginal utility of consumption is constant (as in the previous chapter, where I worked with the indirect utility function).

The derivation of the optimum income tax formula, $T(wL)$, is highly complex, and raises a number of difficult issues. The original paper by Mirrlees contains 141 numbered equations, and here it is only possible to describe some features of his results. In general terms, he characterized the condition which must be satisfied by the marginal tax rate, T', at all points, and an end-point condition.

In the special case considered here, these conditions for optimality take a rather simpler form. The first simplification arises from the fact that the utility function has a zero cross-derivative between L and X. As is shown in Atkinson and Stiglitz (1980: 417), we then require that

$$\frac{T'}{1 - T'} = \frac{U_x\varepsilon^*}{wf(w)} \cdot \int_{w}^{\infty} (1/U_x - \Gamma'/\lambda(\omega)]f(\omega)\,d\omega \tag{3.10}$$

at all w where positive quantities of labour are supplied

where λ is the Lagrange multiplier associated with the revenue constraint, ω is a variable of integration, and we define

$$\varepsilon^* \equiv 1 + \frac{LU_{LL}}{U_L} \tag{3.11}$$

U_X denotes the marginal utility of income, and this is the second simplification, since with the particular cardinalization, it is constant. The absence of an income effect also means that ε^* is equal to $1 + 1/\varepsilon(w)$, where $\varepsilon(w)$ is the substitution elasticity (see Atkinson and Stiglitz 1980: 418 n.). Introducing $\phi(w)$ for the social marginal utility of income accruing to a person with wage rate w, normalized by dividing by λ, we arrive at the condition

$$\frac{T'}{1 - T'} = \left[1 + \frac{1}{\varepsilon(w)}\right] \cdot \left[\frac{1 - F(w)}{wf(w)}\right] \cdot [1 - \text{average } \phi \text{ above } w]$$

(3.12)

at all w where positive quantities of labour are supplied

This is coupled with the end-point condition that the average value of ϕ taken over the whole population should be equal to unity. This latter condition is that which results from varying the level of the basic income.

How can these conditions for the optimum tax rate be interpreted? On the right hand side of (3.12), there are four elements. The first is the elasticity of labour supply, which we have extensively discussed in Chapters 1 and 2. As before, the larger the elasticity, the smaller, other things equal, should be the marginal tax rate. What is different here is that the marginal tax rate should be reduced for subgroups of the population where there are reasons to believe that taxes are a more serious disincentive to work. (We have not at this point set ε constant.) This means that empirically we need estimates not just of the elasticity but also as to how it varies with the wage rate.

In some empirical research, the elasticity does indeed vary systematically across the population. The study by Browning and Johnson (1984) assumes an elasticity for the lowest quintile group which is twice that for the fourth quintile group (0.5 compared with 0.25 in round numbers). In terms of formula (3.12), this would mean that an optimum tax rate of 40 per cent for the latter group would correspond to an optimum rate of 29 per cent for the lowest quintile group. More generally, it may be argued that those in the upper earnings ranges are more influenced by tax rates, for example because there is a greater prevalence of self-employment. This would operate in the opposite direction. On the other hand, the labour force participation decision may be more sensitive than that concerning hours of work, or effort, and this may apply to married women found lower down the earnings range. Low initial marginal rates of tax may be designed to avoid discouraging such participation.

The second element in the optimum tax formula is $wf(w)$, which is an indicator of the extent of earnings at the wage level w. The marginal tax rate should be lower, again other things equal, where there are less earnings potentially affected. Such a statement might appear to border on the obvious, but it is rarely made in public finance textbooks. This term depends on the shape of the distribution of wage rates and, although weighted by w, the product $wf(w)$ may be expected to fall as we reach the upper part of the distribution. This would indicate a higher marginal rate of tax on high earners.

These two factors may be seen as embodying efficiency aspects. The third and fourth terms incorporate distributional concerns. To begin with, the case for increasing the marginal tax rate depends on the proportion of the population *above* w. A high marginal tax rate as such performs no valuable distributional function. Its purpose is to increase the *average* tax rates higher up the scale. The pay-off in raising the marginal rate at w depends on how many people are above w. As w gets larger, the pay-off falls, and it reaches zero in the limit. Indeed, where the distribution is bounded, it can be shown that the marginal tax rate at the top should be zero (Seade 1977). This may seem rather surprising, but if there is no one above a particular point, then a positive marginal rate serves no function.

The case for raising the average rate of tax depends on the distributional values, and these are represented by the last term in (3.12). If the government is indifferent with respect to the distribution of income, then $\phi(w)$ is constant for all w, and hence by the end-point condition is equal to 1. It follows that the last term in (3.12) is zero everywhere, and we have a zero tax rate. Where the social marginal utility of income $\phi(w)$ falls with w, then the last term is positive, but the implications depend on the precise form of social objectives.

3.4 Optimum Tax Structure and Differing Objectives

Whether or not the optimum tax rate involves significantly varying tax rates depends therefore on the form of social objectives. And it does so in a way that is not entirely self-evident. In order to explore this, let us take the distributional objectives described in Chapter 2, and the case of the constant labour supply elasticity (as in Atkinson 1990).

Charitable Conservative and Rawlsian Objectives

Suppose that we start with the charitable conservative position, interpreted to mean that the government is concerned with the bottom μ of the population, giving them a weight ϕ_0/ρ, compared to ϕ_0 for the rest of the population (as illustrated in the second part of Figure 2.1). The condition that, on average, the social marginal valuation is equal to unity requires that

$$(1 - \mu)\phi_0 + \frac{\mu\phi_0}{\rho} = 1 \qquad (3.13)$$

For those in the upper $(1 - \mu)$ of the population, the last term in the optimum tax formula (3.12) is then equal to $(1 - \phi_0)$, where this can be calculated as a function of μ and ρ from (3.13).

Where the labour supply elasticity is constant, the variation of the optimum marginal tax rate with w depends solely on

$$\frac{1 - F(w)}{wf(w)} \qquad (3.14)$$

In the special case where the upper part of the distribution follows the Pareto distribution (equation 2.21), this term is constant and equal to $1/\beta$. In this case, the optimum tax rate for all those above the bottom π of the population is constant. Taking the parameter values used in Table 2.2 ($\varepsilon = 0.3$ and $\beta = 3$), and assuming that the government is concerned with the bottom 15 per cent of the population, we can calculate the optimum tax rate to be 6 per cent where $\rho = 0.75$, 16 per cent where $\rho = 0.5$, and 31 per cent where $\rho = 0.25$. These values are lower than those in row 1 of Table 2.2, but no direct comparison can be made, since we have no dependent population.

If the Pareto distribution holds throughout the range of w, then we can show that the optimum tax rate for those in the bottom group is equal to that calculated above times

$$\frac{F(w)}{1 - F(w)} \bigg/ \frac{\mu}{1 - \mu} \qquad (3.15)$$

This expression starts at zero and rises to 1 as $F(w)$ reaches μ, so that the marginal tax rate is increasing over the range of distributional concern. At least at lower incomes, in this case there is justification for a graduated rate structure of the usual kind.

As ρ tends to zero in equation (3.13), we have a version of the Rawlsian objective, where the maximand is the welfare of a bottom *group*, not simply the least advantaged individual. Although the latter interpretation has been applied in the optimum taxation literature (see for example Atkinson 1973), Rawls himself wrote of the 'least fortunate group' and refers to it as a 'limited aggregative principle' (1971: 98), in contrast to thinking of literally the worst-off individual. In his brief discussion of practical implementation, he instanced definitions based on either those with less than the average income of unskilled workers or those with less than half of median income. It is not clear whether he considered the implications of adopting a definition which allowed the least favoured group to be empty (as where everyone has income of at least half the median). The alternative considered here, treating the least advantaged as the bottom μ of the population, does not have this property. From the earlier results, we can see that on this interpretation the Rawlsian tax rate on all except the least favoured group is given by, in the case of the Pareto distribution

$$\frac{T'}{1 - T'} = \frac{1 + 1/\varepsilon}{\beta} \qquad (3.16)$$

With the parameter values used above, this gives a value of 59 per cent. At first, it may appear surprising that the Rawlsian objective does not support graduated rates, but it is a consequence of the fact that this objective is not concerned with the distribution among those not in the least favoured group. The Rawlsian objective is a special case of the charitable conservative position. Reduction in inequality among the top $(1 - \mu)$ is of no interest.

The results described above depend critically on the assumption about the shape of the wage distribution. If we replace the assumption of a Pareto distribution by that of a lognormal distribution, then $(1 - F(w))/wf(w)$ falls with w, tending in the limit to zero as w tends to infinity. Such a conclusion is like that which shows in the case of a distribution with a finite upper bound that there should be a zero marginal tax rate at the top (see, for example, Seade 1977). It indicates that there is indeed an argument for variable marginal rates, but in the reverse direction from that typically found.

Attractive though such a conclusion may be to those who wish to cut top tax rates, they need to be treated with caution. The finite distribution result is only relevant when we are confident that we know the highest wage rate. Where w tends to infinity, the limiting behaviour may be a poor approximation even for the top percentiles, as observed by Mirrlees (1976: 340). In the present case, we may note that, where f is the lognormal distribution, then $(1 - F(w))/wf(w)$ ($\equiv R(w)$) is the Mills ratio (Kendall and Stuart 1969: 137, or Pudney 1989: 303),

Table 3.1 Optimum marginal tax rate with lognormal distribution and different distributional objectives

Percentiles of wage distribution	Rawlsian	$\rho = 0.25$	$\rho = 0.5$	$\rho = 0.75$	Rank order
Median	84.4	62.7	41.4	20.5	73.0
Upper quartile	77.4	51.5	30.8	14.0	71.9
Top decile	71.2	43.4	24.4	10.5	69.0
95%	67.8	39.5	21.5	9.1	66.7
Top percentile	62.0	33.6	17.5	7.2	61.7
99.9%	56.3	28.5	14.4	5.8	56.2

Note: $\varepsilon = 0.3$ and $\mu = 0.15$.

which is widely used in micro-econometrics. From the tables of this ratio, we can calculate the optimum marginal tax rate in the charitable conservative case, and the results are shown in Table 3.1 for different percentile points of the distribution. These results confirm that zero is a poor approximation even for the top 0.1 per cent, but show how the optimum tax rate declines rather than increases in this case of a lognormal wage distribution.

Redistributive Preferences

It is therefore interesting to contrast the charitable conservative position with a more redistributive set of values. Suppose that we adopt the rank order weights, such that, where they are on average equal to unity,

$$\phi = 2[1 - F(w)] \tag{3.17}$$

The net social marginal valuation declines linearly with $F(w)$ from twice the average for the lowest-paid worker to approach zero as w tends to infinity. Evaluating the last term in the optimum tax condition (3.12), we can see that this is equal to $F(w)$, so that this distributional term rises from zero to unity. The overall pattern of the optimum marginal tax rates depends on the shape of the wage distribution. With the Pareto distribution, we have

$$\frac{T'}{1 - T'} = \frac{(1 + 1/\varepsilon)F(w)}{\beta} \tag{3.18}$$

Where the Pareto distribution applies throughout the range, the optimum marginal tax rate rises from 0 to the Rawlsian value as w tends to infinity. In the case of the lognormal distribution, we have the same expression with $1/\beta$ replaced by $R(w)$, the Mills ratio. Multiplied by $F(w)$, this declines less rapidly, as may be seen from the last column in Table 3.1.

3.5 Categorical Benefits

The second feature of the SI/GT structure is that social insurance benefits are paid related to people who qualify by virtue of satisfying a specified categorical condition or conditions. Sickness benefit is paid to those who are off work on account of ill-health, and for those unable to work in the long term there are invalidity or disablement benefits. Old age pensions may be paid to those who have reached a certain age (65 in the United Kingdom). Unemployment benefit, under certain conditions, is paid in most countries to those who have lost their jobs, are available for work, and are actively seeking employment.

In order to examine the implications of such a categorical payment, I return to the situation considered in Chapter 2 where there is a subgroup who have zero earnings potential and who constitute a fraction μ of the population. Moreover, let us also return to the situation where there is a flat tax rate and basic income. We can then consider whether or not there should be a categorical social insurance payment, I, to the sick and retired, in addition to the basic income, B. The objective function becomes

$$\mu\,\Gamma\{v[B + I]\} + \int_{w_0}^{\infty}\Gamma\{V[w(1 - t), B]\}f(w)dw \tag{3.19}$$

and the budget constraint

$$B + \mu I = t\int_{w_0}^{\infty}wL\,dF\,(w) - R \tag{3.20}$$

Formulated in this way, an increase in I raises social welfare where the social marginal value of income to the dependent population exceeds the average net social marginal valuation of income for the population as a whole. There are two reasons why we may expect this condition to be satisfied, and hence for some categorical transfer to be desirable: (i) the welfare level of the dependent population is lower, so that I is better targeted than B, although this clearly depends on the level of I; the social insurance transfer may reach a level at which the sick and retired are better off than the average worker; (ii) for those in work the *net* social marginal valuation is lower where a lump-sum transfer leads them to reduce their labour supply (for a labour supply function which allows income effects), whereas for the dependent population there are no adverse labour supply effects. It follows that where these conditions hold a small categorical transfer will certainly be desirable.

This finding was reported by Akerlof (1978) in terms of the advantages of 'tagging' in improving the efficiency of redistribution. It may also be seen as an application of the Le Chatelier principle, in that additional instruments can only improve the level of social welfare; it is always open to the government to set the categorical benefit at zero.

3.6 Concluding Comments

The comparison of a simple BI/FT with a categorical benefit/ graduated tax alternative illustrates some of the relevant considerations, but may also serve to highlight what is missing from the analysis. An obvious omission is the cost of administration. The introduction of further parameters into the tax-benefit system is not costless. One of the arguments for the flat tax is that it greatly simplifies administration for government, taxpayers, and third parties such as employers. This may come about through simplification of the individual tax return: the cover to Hall and Rabushka's *The Flat Tax* (1985) shows their simplified form which they claim could fit on a postcard. In this context much of the saving in administrative cost comes from the fact that it would not be necessary to police *who* receives particular income. (The BI/FT would be even simpler than the Hall–Rabushka plan in that the personal allowances would also be abolished.)

Alternatively, the move to a flat tax would allow tax revenue to be collected at source without the need for adjustments at the individual level. All wage income, all interest, dividends, and rent, and all transfer payments would be paid subject to deduction at the single rate. In this situation, the introduction of a dual rate would involve the cost of the establishment of a procedure for calculating total income for each taxpayer, or at least establishing that no higher rate tax was due/verifying claims for the 'subsidy' on high earnings.

Administrative costs are only one of several considerations missing from the earlier treatment. If policy-makers are surprised at the possibility that marginal rates should fall rather than rise with income, then it may be that they have not thought of the argument described earlier, or it may be that there are other considerations which enter their judgements. These are taken up in the next chapter.

4 Liberty and Public Choice Theory

4.1 Introduction

The optimum tax approach studied in Chapters 2 and 3 has, in my judgement, contributed substantially to furthering our understanding of the issues involved in the design of taxation and income maintenance. By posing the government's problem in a precise manner, it has allowed us to clarify the role of different considerations and the way in which they are inter-related. The general notion of a trade-off between equity and efficiency, which one finds in what Aaron calls the 'old-time religion of public finance' (1989: 10), takes on a concrete form in the equations set out in the previous chapters. At the same time, the analysis, in becoming more precise, has tended to focus on a part of the picture to the exclusion of other elements. For this, the optimum tax literature has quite reasonably been criticized.

In this chapter I consider two main lines of criticism. The first is that the optimum tax literature, concerned with a government which maximizes social welfare, takes too narrow a view of the objectives of policy. We need to consider other objectives. Account has been taken in our earlier analysis of the possibility that different people may have different distributional values (different values of γ for example), but we must also recognize that a single person may apply several different criteria when judging policy options. There may in this sense be a *plurality* of values. The second objection, associated particularly with the public choice school, is that the optimum tax analysis fails to take account of the way in which tax and benefit policy is actually formed. No attempt is made here to provide a full review of the public choice literature, which under the influence of Buchanan, Tullock, and others has grown extensively, but in the second part of this chapter (Sections 4.6 and 4.7) I consider the implications for the design of policy. In particular, I suggest one way of bringing together the optimum tax and public choice approaches.

4.2 A Plurality of Objectives

In Chapters 2 and 3, I considered the design of tax and benefit policy from the standpoint of a government concerned to maximize a social welfare function which depended on individual welfares. Social judgements entered in the form of the weighting attached to the welfare of different people, and, while this was not necessarily based on private valuations (as with the rank order weights), the effect of policy was assessed solely in terms of the impact on the welfare of individuals.

In the first part of this chapter, I consider the implications of extending the range of objectives to include *non-welfarist* principles: i.e. those which are not based solely on considerations of individual welfare, as conventionally understood. The main example that I use is that there may be concern about individual freedom or liberty. This example comes naturally to mind in view of the developments in Eastern Europe, where such considerations are likely to be to the fore in the design of the public finance system. But in view of the importance of liberty as a political value in the development of modern societies it is interesting to speculate why it has not played a more central role in the discussion of the issues of public finance. The other examples considered here are (i) the objective of avoiding 'dependency', or assuring individual independence, and (ii) the idea that people 'deserve' to receive their just reward for effort.

The objectives of securing individual freedom, avoiding dependency, or rewarding effort do not *replace* concern for the welfare of individuals. Rather we have now to recognize that we have a plurality of principles. This concept of plurality refers not to the fact different people may disagree but to the conflict of values to be found within one person. As it is put by Williams,

A characteristic dispute about values in society, such as some issue of equality against freedom, is not one most typically enacted by a body of single-minded egalitarians confronting a body of equally single-minded libertarians, but is rather a conflict which one person, equipped with a more generous range of human values, could find enacted in himself. (Williams 1981: 73)

It is with the implications of this 'more generous range of human values' than assumed in the optimum tax analysis that I am now concerned.

The plurality of objectives in turn raises two important questions. First, there is the relation between different principles. If there is a plurality of objectives, then how are they combined in reaching a final decision? The second issue which arises when we depart from a purely social welfare approach is that non-welfarist objectives tend to be more ambiguous in their interpretation.

The problem of interpretation applies especially to objectives, such as freedom, which are naturally defined at a higher, and more general, level of discourse and which are less easily translated to the particular context with which I am concerned here: the case for a basic income/flat tax scheme, and the comparison with a social insurance/graduated tax structure. In Chapter 1, I considered one possible interpretation of liberty in terms of freedom of choice. Following Lindbeck (1988), we may consider that high marginal tax rates cause people to be 'trapped' in a certain income bracket, with very little possibility of changing their economic situation by their own effort. On the other hand, rather different interpretations have been given, and two of these are discussed in the next two sections. The ideas of dependency and desert are the subject of Section 4.5.

A Hierarchy of Principles

In the rest of this section, I concentrate on the problem of combining multiple criteria, taking as an illustration concerns about liberty and about social welfare. One possible resolution of the problem—that mainly considered below—is that the principles are ordered in a hierarchy. For instance, non-welfare considerations impose one or more *prior constraints* on the choice of tax and social security policy. Social welfare maximization is pursued subject to such a constraint(s). The prior consideration is always whether or not the constraint is satisfied; a policy may score well in terms of social welfare, but not even be considered because it fails to satisfy the prior constraint. We have in effect a *lexicographic* ordering (as in a dictionary with the first letter having priority, and then the second letter), with the non-welfare considerations having to be satisfied first, and only then social welfare being the guide to policy choice.

Perhaps the most celebrated example of such a lexicographic approach is to be found in the theory of justice of Rawls (1971). As already noted, the Rawlsian concern with the least advantaged, or the difference principle, is subject to a prior liberty principle, which requires that the state achieve the maximal level of liberty equal for all. Although economists (myself included: for example, Atkinson 1973) have tended to concentrate on the difference principle, Rawls insists that the liberty principle has to be met before the least-advantaged criterion is brought into play. At the outset, he states the two principles as follows:

First: each person is to have an equal right to the most extensive basic liberty compatible with a similar liberty for others.

Second: social and economic inequalities are to be arranged so that they are both (a) reasonably expected to be to everyone's advantage, and (b) attached to positions and offices open to all. . . . These principles are to be arranged in a serial order with the first principle prior to the second. This ordering means that a departure from the institutions of equal liberty . . . cannot be justified by, or compensated for, by greater social and economic advantages. (Rawls 1971: 60–1)

On this basis, if the taxes indicated by maximizing the welfare of the least advantaged violate the equal liberty principle, then they are ruled out. Only levels and structures of taxation that satisfy the liberty principle can be considered.

A Higher-Order Maximand

Such a lexicographic approach to combining the different principles is not the only one conceivable. An alternative possibility is that the different considerations, social welfare included, are traded off, one against the other, in a higher-level social maximand. This appears to have been envisaged in the work of

John Stuart Mill, where he talks of a higher-level 'umpire' between different objectives. To quote from his *A System of Logic*,

There must be some standard by which to determine the goodness or badness, absolute and comparative, of ends, or objects of desire. And whatever that standard is, there can be but one: for if there were several ultimate principles of conduct, the same conduct might be approved by one of those principles and condemned by another; and there would be needed some more general principle, as umpire between them. (1843: 554–5)

Similarly, Griffin in his book on *Well-Being* argues that liberalism should not be defended by saying that it is incommensurate with other values:

If liberty is to be defended, it has to be taken down from the shaky perch of 'incomparability' and placed in the same domain as other prudential values, where they will conflict, where none is above the fray, where some, however, are weighty enough usually to win a conflict, and where even, occasionally, a weighty value can assume in a particular case such weight that no amount of some lightweight value can overcome it. (1986: 91–2)

What are likely to be the implications of admitting the possibility of such trade-offs? In the present context of concerns with both liberty and social welfare, such a Millian 'umpire' may for example give different priorities depending on the level of development of the country attained. At very low levels of existence, individual survival may have priority over concern with liberties; on the other hand, once subsistence is assured, priority may be given to liberty.

As Barry (1973) has argued, even Rawls accepts that there may be a trade-off. Late in *A Theory of Justice*, Rawls states that

The lexical ordering of the two principles is the long-run tendency of the general conception of justice consistently pursued under reasonably favourable conditions. . . . as the conditions of civilization improve, the marginal significance for our good of further economic and social advantages diminishes relative to the interests of liberty. (1971: 542)

Beyond some level of development, according to Rawls, liberty becomes, and remains, the prior principle. Applied to the policy issue considered here, this may appear to mean that the case for a basic income is stronger in less developed economies; however, such a conclusion depends critically on the interpretation of liberty, as discussed later in this chapter.

Resort to a higher-order maximand raises the question as to whether—once we introduce Mill's umpire—we are not back with a single objective function? The answer may be 'yes', but this does not vitiate the approach, since the crucial issue is the *form* of this maximand. The trading-off of liberty and social welfare, for example, takes account of the distinctive features of both. As it is put by Sen and Williams in the context of rights, 'even when trade-offs are permitted, rights of different . . . types do not get merged into one homogeneous total . . . if they are combined—and even scaled against each other in terms of moral importance—this aggregation is *within* an essentially pluralist approach' (1982: 19). Hurley gives an example as to how a pluralist theory, including considerations of both total welfare and of equality of resources, can be represented as maximizing a single magnitude, but emphasizes that none the less 'A distinction remains between theories that are pluralistic in [a] substantive sense and theories of which the substance, and not merely the form, is monistic' (1989: 269–70).

Values in Conflict

A third position is that there may be unavoidable conflict between different principles:

Isaiah Berlin has always insisted that there is a plurality of values which can conflict with one another, and which are not reducible to one another; consequently, that we cannot conceive of a situation in which it was true that all value-conflict had been eliminated, and that there had been no loss of value on the way. (Williams 1981: 71)

An example of such a possible conflict is that identified by Sen (1970) between a condition of personal liberty, allowing each person to be decisive over one distinct pair of alternatives, and the Pareto principle which requires that a social decision not be made in favour of X when there is an alternative Y judged everyone to be better or no worse.

Conflict between principles can lead to *incompleteness* in social judgements. Suppose that we were to conclude that an adequate basic income, requiring a sizeable increase in tax rates, would achieve significantly greater social welfare but at the expense of significantly infringing individual liberty. We may then be unable to reach a conclusion as to its desirability. One principle may point in one direction, but another in the opposite direction. For economists, accustomed to the incompleteness of the Lorenz ranking of income distributions, this may appear quite natural. As it is put by Sen,

Intelligent moral choice demands that we not choose . . . an alternative that we can see is morally inferior to another feasible alternative. But this does not require that the chosen alternative be seen to be 'best' . . . , since there may be no best alternative at all, given the incompleteness of our moral ranking. (Sen 1985: 181)

The problem when considering a radical reform such as the BI/FT scheme is that incompleteness appears to favour the status quo. If there is one principle according to which the reform is inferior, then this is grounds for blocking any change, regardless of its merits when viewed according to other criteria. As a result, 'more is needed, if the pluralist is not to spend too much of his time as a rueful spectator of political change which is itself powered by forces which either have nothing to do with values at all, or else which express value-claims more exclusive than the pluralist himself would admit' (Williams 1981: 71). This was written before the 1980s and for those who witnessed with misgivings the actions of the Thatcher government in the United Kingdom, the passage must strike a chord.

There are, therefore, at least three ways of viewing the relationship between different principles, and these should be borne in mind when considering the alternatives to social welfare maximization considered in the next three sections.

4.3 Liberty and Voluntary Participation

It is not straightforward to translate the principle of liberty to the narrowly defined economic problem considered here. There are a number of ways in which liberty can be interpreted, and they may lead us to draw very different conclusions. In this, and the next section, I have chosen two distinctive and contrasting interpretations.

I begin with the approach of Buchanan, who invokes the Wicksell–Lindahl concept of the state as a voluntary exchange, and regards the liberties of taxpayers as having been infringed if they would prefer to exit from the present fiscal regime and set up an alternative fiscal regime. As such, his approach is concerned more with average than with marginal tax rates, it being the burden of financing redistribution that leads richer taxpayers to wish to leave. In his discussion of Rawls, Buchanan interprets the liberty principle in the following terms: 'the idealised internal exit option places ethical limits on the absolute level of taxation and it is only within the limits that the second Rawlsian principle, or indeed any other distributional principle, can be legitimately applied' (1984: 108). The reason that this constraint allows *some* redistribution is that there are fixed costs of financing the state, and providing certain public goods, which would have to be duplicated by the rich if they chose the exit option.

The process is illustrated by Buchanan in terms of a numerical example of a two-class society (see also Buchanan and Faith 1987). There are two types of worker: 25 of type X, who are each twice as productive as each of the 50 type Y, producing two units to their one. There are no disincentive effects, and total output is 100. The minimum cost of providing the legal-protective framework of the state is ten units, regardless of the number of inhabitants.

Suppose that the state were to levy a tax at a high rate (Buchanan takes a rate of 90 per cent) and use the proceeds in excess of ten units (the cost of the legal-protective services) to finance a uniform basic income. With a tax rate of 90 per cent, the total available is $90 - 10 = 80$, divided among 75 people gives 1.067 units basic income. The net position of each type is:

X gross income   = 2, after tax = 0.2,
    plus basic income = 1.267
Y gross income   = 1, after tax = 0.1,
    plus basic income = 1.167

In this case, the group X can clearly do better by establishing a separate state, generating a total income of 50, without the basic income. The cost of the legal-protective services are now higher per head, but can be financed by a tax at the rate of 20 per cent. Buchanan concludes that 'The ninety percent level of taxation is *not* ethically justifiable on the principle of maximal liberty' (1984: 109). The same applies to any tax rate which leaves the X workers with a net income of less than 1.6 (i.e. 2 less a tax rate of 20 per cent). There is therefore an upper limit to·the tax rate in the full economy, containing both X and Y workers, that satisfies the liberty principle.

This example serves to bring out the central idea; at the same time, the two-class assumption means that some important factors are not taken into account. To spell out the argument a little further, let us set the discussion in the context of the model considered in Chapters 2 and 3, where there is a continuous distribution of people with different wage rates, w, but where we disregard incentive effects, each person supplying one unit of labour (the labour supply elasticity $\varepsilon = 0$ and $L_0 = 1$). (For simplicity, I assume also that there are no sick or disabled, so that $\mu = 0$.) Suppose that there is a fixed cost of the legal-protection services of the state, equal to a proportion r of the total economy earnings ($E\{w\}$ in the notation of Chapter 2), assumed to be less than the ratio of the lowest wage, w_0, to the average.

If one now imagines coalitions of increasing size, beginning with those with the highest wage rates and working progressively down the distribution, then exit to a 'no-redistribution state' would not be an option until the coalition reached a certain finite size, in the sense that the total earnings, and hence maximum tax revenue, would be less than required to finance the fixed cost. There is some wage rate at which the maximum revenue equals that required, and the necessary tax rate to finance the no-redistribution state then falls as the size of the coalition increases. (Feasibility is by assumption assured when all belong to the coalition.)

The liberty of an individual with wage rate w is said on the Buchanan principle to be infringed if he would prefer to join a no-redistribution coalition containing all those with wage rates greater than or equal to w. There remains, however, the question as to how the tax burden is distributed among members of the coalition, who have differing interests. Suppose for example that the tax is a uniform poll tax, T, which has to finance the legal-protection services:

$$T(1 - F(w)) = rE\{w\} \tag{4.1}$$

the left-hand side being the revenue collected from the proportion, $(1 - F(w))$, of the population who belong to the coalition. The value of T is plotted as a function of w, and hence of the size of the coalition, in Figure 4.1; its shape depends on the form of the distribution. By assumption, the lowest-wage person can afford to pay the poll tax (equal to $rE\{w\}$ if everyone is in the coalition); and the smallest feasible coalition is given by the intersection of T with the 45° line, which gives total earnings.

Comparing the exit option with the BI/FT, we can see that the latter means that the person pays net tax of

$$tw - (t - r)E\{w\} = t(w - E\{w\}) + rE\{w\} \tag{4.2}$$

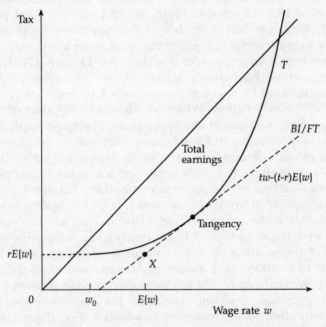

Fig. 4.1 Upper limit to tax rate imposed by internal exit option

For those with wages below the average, this is less than the poll tax T, since the latter is at least as great as $rE\{w\}$. The net position with the BI/FT is shown in Figure 4.1 by the dashed line. Its slope is given by t, and different values correspond to different lines pivoting about the point X. The liberty principle constrains the tax rate to be less than the value which is just tangent to the T curve (the highest acceptable tax rate is that shown).

This presentation of the argument, however, begs a number of questions. The assumption that the hypothetical no-redistribution alternative would levy a uniform poll tax could be replaced by the assumption that the tax would be proportional (as in Buchanan's account). This would make adhesion to the coalition more attractive to the marginal member. As is noted by Buchanan and Faith (1987: 1025 n.), the hypothetical government may be expected itself to follow the liberty principle in determining the pattern of taxation. This issue did not arise in the two-class example.

A more serious qualification concerns the precise specification of the exit option. From the literature on local public goods we know that in models of this type there are problems of the non-existence of equilibrium, analogous to the emptiness of the core (Atkinson and Stiglitz 1980, Lecture 17). In our discussion of Buchanan's argument, we considered only a particular kind of coalition—one formed by the richest x per cent of the population. When we allow for any kind of coalition, which is surely in the spirit of the liberty principle, then there may exist no BI/FT scheme which cannot be improved upon by some group forming a no-redistribution state. This is purely conjecture, but what is needed is a rigorous analysis of the implications of the internal exit option. Put another way, the definition of an allocation which is proof against internal exit needs to be made precise. What exactly are the options that we have to consider? There needs to be further investigation of the relation, if any, with other game-theoretic treatments of taxation, such as that of Aumann and Kurz (1977).

The internal exit option has been discussed in relation to the BI/FT proposal; it is not clear how the same considerations influence the Social Insurance/Graduated Tax alternative. It could be argued that social insurance, while compulsory, involves a connection between contributions and future benefits. The lifetime reallocation has a firmer contractual basis than with the purely tax-financed basic income, and this enters the internal exit calculation in the same way as it may affect actual migration decisions. It seems possible that social insurance involves less of a conflict with the principle of liberty, although such a position only makes sense if we see the issue as a matter of degree rather than in terms of absolutes.

The Buchanan model imposes an upper limit on the tax rate that may be levied; this limit is likely to be greater than zero, reflecting the positive advantage provided by sharing the fixed costs of government. There are, however, those who argue that no taxation at all can be consistent with individual liberty. According to Nozick, 'taxation of earnings from labour is on a par with forced labour' (1974: 169). For those who take this position, only a minimal, nightwatchman state is justified, and neither a basic income nor social insurance would have any role.

The approach considered in this section may be seen as an application of the principle of *negative* liberty, in the sense that it requires the absence of constraints on individual behaviour. This is indeed in the tradition of the voluntary participation theory of public finance. A different tradition, however, that based on ideas of a national minimum, would point to a different interpretation. Following the common, if controversial, distinction in the literature on political philosophy, we may contrast negative and *positive* freedoms. Positive freedom requires not simply the absence of constraints but also that people are able to make effective use of their civil and political liberties (see, for example, Sen 1988). This is explored in the next section.

4.4 Positive Liberty and the Basic Income as Safety Net

The previous analysis saw the basic income as being in conflict with individual freedom, with the latter principle imposing a maximum to the tax rate which can be levied. There are, however, supporters of the BI/FT scheme which see it as making a positive contribution to individual liberty. We have therefore to ask whether there are other arguments, indicating an alternative relation between the basic income and liberty.

One such argument is provided by the different interpretation of the Rawlsian liberty principle given by Barry (1973). He argues that basic liberty (such as political and legal freedom) and economic resources are *both* inputs into the production of 'effective liberty'. He notes that, just as a society with no basic liberty has no effective liberty, so too a society with no resources would effectively lack liberty: 'no amount of basic liberty, however great, produces any effective liberty unless it is combined with some fixed minimum level of wealth' (1973: 78). He represents this relationship in stylized form by supposing that the amount of effective liberty is the product of the amount of basic liberty and the amount of resources up to a certain level, after which extra resources do not add to effective liberty. Barry shows how this can lead to a changing relation between different variables as an economy develops. At low levels of development, increases in both basic liberty and economic resources are effective. Beyond a certain point, priority is given to increasing basic liberties, until the maximum liberty is attained, at which point the second Rawlsian principle comes into play.

How is this relevant to the case for a basic income? Here the issue is the *distribution* of resources, not considered in the account just given. It can be argued that it is now in *richer* countries that the basic income comes into its own. Where total resources are sufficient to guarantee maximum effective liberty to all, then priority of liberty requires that the first claim on these resources is to ensure that everyone does indeed secure such maximum liberty. The case for a basic income is that it is an essential *complement* of political and legal freedom; without a minimum level of resources, liberty cannot be effective.

This positive interpretation of liberty is not only different from the negative freedom discussed in the previous section; it may also be in direct conflict. This is well brought out in the following passage by the Webbs:

To the employer and to the landlord . . . all this enforcement of a 'National Minimum' . . . loomed as a limitation of his personal freedom. . . . But the other side of the shield, seen by the wage-earner as the outcome of this same legislation, is an enormous growth in practical freedom of action, a liberty positively enlarged by law. (1911: 321)

From this other side of the shield, liberty requires a minimum of material goods in order that people may effectively participate in society. To give a simple example, the electoral registration system in Britain is related to household residence and it is much more difficult for the homeless to participate in the democratic process.

This notion of participation underlies much of recent work on poverty in advanced countries, such as that of Townsend (1979 and 1993): for example,

Poverty may best be understood as applying not just to those who are victims of a maldistribution of resources but, more exactly, to those whose resources do not allow them to fulfil the elaborate social demands and customs which have been placed upon citizens of that society. (1993: 36)

The notion is related to that of 'social exclusion' which is receiving a great deal of attention in the European Union, as illustrated by the statement of the Council of Ministers of the European Community in launching the Second Poverty Programme that the poor are those 'whose resources (material, cultural and social) are so limited as to exclude them from the minimum acceptable way of life in the Member State in which they live' (Commission of the European Communities 1989: 9). It should be stressed that such concern for exclusion does not follow from the standard welfare economic formulation of objectives, which attaches no particular significance to any level of resources. Put another way, considerations of exclusion enter the Rawlsian analysis via the liberty principle not via the difference principle.

The basic income may be seen in this way as providing a *social safety net* to prevent social exclusion or to ensure that people can participate freely in society. As such, the objective enjoys support from a wide constituency. It is for example a declared objective of the International Monetary Fund that structural adjustment plans, and the programme for transition to a market economy, should set in place a social safety net, so as to safeguard the position of the poor. Where, however, there is less agreement is in the *rationale* of the safety net, and this has major implications for its design. There are in fact at least two different interpretations of the positive freedom argument for a basic income (Goodin 1988). The first is concerned with the freedom of the poor themselves, and this was the interpretation implicit in the presentation of the argument above. The second is concerned with the freedom of the *rest of the population*. The non-poor may be constrained, or perceive themselves to be constrained, in their actions by the existence of the poor population. The non-poor might, for example, prefer to scale down the welfare state but feel unable to do so while some section of the population remains dependent on its services. As Hayek says of a national minimum, 'The necessity of some such arrangement in an industrial society is unquestioned—be it only in the interest of those who require protection against acts of desperation on the part of the needy' (1960: 285). Put more generously, the provision of a social safety net legitimizes the pursuit of other objectives.

This distinction between different justifications for the basic income as a national minimum becomes important when we consider the design of the safety net in more detail. In particular, should safety net payments be paid unconditionally or should they depend on availability and willingness to work? The typical social insurance or social assistance scheme is highly conditional: to qualify for unemployment insurance, one has, for example, be available for work and willing to take employment offered. In contrast, the basic income is unconditional, and this lack of conditionality is seen as important from the standpoint of guaranteeing the effective liberty of those dependent on its receipt. However, from the perspective of the non-poor an unconditional benefit may appear unjustified: they may regard the lack of conditionality as generating dependency, to which I now turn.

4.5 Dependency and Deserts

In Chapter 1, I referred to the view of socialists and environmentalists who see the basic income as freeing people from dependence on the market economy. In contrast, those with conservative political views hold that the basic income would in fact *create* dependency on the state. According to this position, it is not acceptable that the basic income should be sufficiently generous that people choose not to supply labour. There should, on this perspective, be a side-constraint that labour supply be positive even at the lowest wage. Among the reasons given for this are that preferences are endogenous and that attitudes to work will change (as in references to a 'welfare culture').

The implications of the side-constraint that L be positive are readily seen from our earlier analysis. Whether or not it is binding on the BI/FT depends on the form of the labour supply function. With the simple iso-elastic labour supply function used in much of Chapter 2, labour supply remains positive at all positive wage rates (and is unaffected by the level of the basic income). On the other hand, with the linear earnings function set out in the Appendix to Chapter 2, L falls to zero if the wage rate falls below a critical value w_- defined in (A2.3). The side condition is that the lowest wage rate w_0 should be greater than w_-, as indeed I have assumed earlier to be the case. Writing this explicitly, and using the definitions of b' and r' (from A2.5), we have (see A2.7)

$$b' < \frac{(1 - t)w_0}{\delta[E\{w\}/(1 - \mu)]} \qquad (4.3)$$

In terms of the menu of possibilities, plotted in Figure 4.2, the right-hand side of (4.3) is a straight line up to the left from ($t = 1$, $b' = 0$), and the area to the right of this line (i.e. the shaded area) is excluded. As shown, this is not a binding constraint, in that even at the maximum feasible basic income everyone is choosing to work. Indeed, it may not be particularly limiting: taking $\delta = 0.3$ and $\mu = 0.15$, as before, and a zero revenue requirement, if the lowest wage is a quarter of the average, then the upper limit on the tax rate is 90 per cent. There is not necessarily conflict between the socialist and conservative positions. The basic income may on the one hand be considered 'adequate', while on the other not induce people to choose not to supply labour. (This depends of course on the level of the lowest wages, and a minimum wage may here play an important role.)

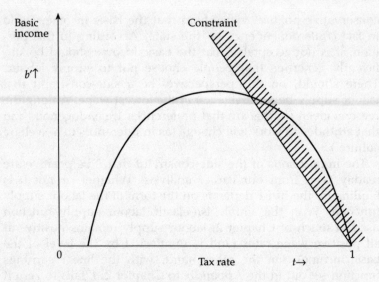

Fig. 4.2 Restriction on BI/FT scheme arising from no-dependency requirement

Where the aim of avoiding dependency is a significant restriction on the basic income, this may be grounds for preferring a social insurance benefit to a basic income. To the extent that those not in the labour force are clearly distinct—which may be more applicable to the handicapped, long-term sick, and the elderly—then a rise in a categorical social insurance benefit does not violate the constraint. Put differently, labour market considerations may lead to the basic income being set at a level which cannot on its own provide adequate income support to those not in the labour force. If this is so, then people concerned with redistribution may prefer the existing social insurance system.

The conservative side of the debate is concerned with dependence *on the state*; the counter-argument of those favouring the basic income is that it would reduce a person's dependence on *other people*. Put the other way, the absence of a guaranteed basic income means that those without adequate earning power are dependent on their partners or their families for support. Cuts in welfare state spending programmes, especially those for young people, in countries such as the United Kingdom have often been accompanied by statements that the family should take a greater degree of financial responsibility, but this increases dependency of a different form.

As noted at the outset of this chapter, non-welfarist objectives tend to be more ambiguous in their interpretation.

Desert

The belief that people should not be dependent on the welfare state may be seen as the counterpart of the view that those contributing to society deserve some degree of reward. Such a *desert* principle has not played a major role in public economics, even though 'most people in present-day Britain . . . hold a view of social justice which gives a large place to making incomes correspond to personal deserts' (Miller 1976: 120). As he discusses in depth, the relationship between social justice and ideas of desert is one of some complexity. Here I confine myself to noting one possible application in the present context. One objection to high marginal rates of tax is that people 'deserve' to retain at least a certain proportion of the earnings gained by extra effort. If the difficulty is ignored of distinguishing between differences in earnings due to extra effort and those due to other factors, then this idea has some resonance in public discussion. In particular, one senses that the strong feelings that surround the poverty trap arise to a considerable extent because it is regarded as 'unfair', since people deserve to be better off through working longer hours.

Considerations of desert may therefore provide a further reason for imposing an upper limit on the marginal tax rate which can be levied. This would limit the level of a basic income. It would affect the analysis of the non-linear income tax. A constraint on the maximum permissible marginal tax rate would lead to a solution consisting of 'blocked' intervals, where the constraint binds, and 'unblocked' intervals, where the previous condition holds. It should be stressed that this argument has nothing to do with work incentives. It is the unfairness of the poverty trap that is the source of concern, not the possibility that it may discourage work effort. This means that the argument does not rest in any way on empirical evidence about work decisions. Moreover, concerns of desert presumably apply with equal force at all points on the income scale. High marginal tax rates applied to the poor are just as objectionable as high rates applied at the top.

4.6 Public Choice

The purpose of the foregoing analysis is to illuminate the structure of arguments, explaining the relationship between instruments, constraints, and objectives. At the same time, as noted in Chapter 1, one must recognize that the constraints include those of political decision-making, and the public choice school has rightly stressed the need to examine the structure within which political decisions are made. We should not overlook the fact that the government itself is an important subject for study. As it was put by Lindahl in 1959,

Why should public finance theory only be allowed to investigate the effects of various tax proposals, but not be permitted to analyze the factors which determine the form they take and the choice between different proposals which is then made by the political authorities? In both cases the question is one of clarifying factual causal relationships. (1959: 8–9)

Public choice theory puts political activity on a par with economic activity, treating the government as an economic actor whose behaviour is to be explained. There is, however, little yet in the way of agreed models of this behaviour. While the utility-maximizing model of individual consumption and labour supply decisions is open to a number of important objections, it nevertheless enjoys a degree of agreement among economists. The same cannot be said of models of political behaviour, where even those which have been widely used are open to serious objections.

Here, I take as an example the most obvious model of the political process, which is that of majority voting. Suppose that we are making a single political decision—like the choice of tax rate under the BI/FT scheme—and that everyone votes between two tax rates on the basis of the resulting level of utility. In reality, of course, voters may be influenced by many other considerations apart from their own personal interest—they may, for instance, have regard to concepts of fairness or justice—but this is not allowed for here. The voter is assumed to perceive correctly the relation between tax rates and government revenue, anticipating the reactions of taxpayers to taxation. This has been described by Meltzer and Richard (1981) as a 'rational' theory of government behaviour, although, as elsewhere in economics, the term promises more than it delivers.

Under certain conditions, the majority voting outcome is determinate and corresponds to the tax rate chosen by the *median voter*. One set of circumstances where the median voter theorem applies is that where individual preferences are *single-peaked*: for each person the level of utility associated with different tax rates is an inverse-U shape, or has a corner maximum with no other turning-point. (In fact, in the case of the linear income tax, it is sufficient that a weaker condition hold: that preferences be such that we can order people by income independently of the tax schedule (Roberts 1977).)

Where the median voter theorem applies, it is possible to relate the politically chosen tax rate to such factors as the elasticity of labour supply, the extent to which other revenue has to be raised, the degree of inequality in the distribution of wages and the proportion of the population unable to work. In the case of the special iso-elastic labour supply model, a voter with wage rate w ranks the different tax rates according to the level of indirect utility, which is proportional to

$$t(1 - t)^{\varepsilon} + \frac{(1 - t)^{1+\varepsilon}}{1 + \varepsilon} \cdot \frac{w^{1+\varepsilon}}{E\{w^{1+\varepsilon}\}} - \frac{r}{1 - \mu} \qquad (4.4)$$

(obtained using (2.5) and (2.16) and dividing the level of indirect utility by $L_0 E\{w^{1+\varepsilon}\}$). Differentiating with respect to t,

$$\frac{\partial V}{\partial t} \sim (1 - t)^{\varepsilon}\left[1 - \frac{w^{1+\varepsilon}}{E\{w^{1+\varepsilon}\}}\right] - \frac{\varepsilon t}{1 - t} \qquad (4.5)$$

Everyone with earnings ($w^{1+\varepsilon} L_0$) above the average for the working population prefers the tax rate to be set at zero (assuming that it cannot be negative); for those with earnings below this level, there is a preferred tax rate given by

$$\frac{1}{1-t} = \frac{1}{\varepsilon} \cdot \left[1 - \frac{w^{1+\varepsilon}}{E\{w^{1+\varepsilon}\}} \right] \tag{4.6}$$

(which could be obtained from the condition (2.15) for the optimum tax rate by concentrating the weight ϕ at w and setting it zero elsewhere). It may be seen that the preferred tax rate declines with the elasticity of labour supply.

If there were no dependent population ($\mu = 0$), and if the distribution of earnings were symmetric, then the median voter would prefer a zero tax rate. If, however, the median level of earnings is less than the mean, as with the lognormal distribution, then the median voter supports the introduction of a BI/FT scheme. Since the dependent population all support such a scheme, up to the point where B is maximized, the larger μ, the higher the tax rate chosen. Suppose that the elasticity is 0.3. Then, if the median voter has earnings equal to 85 per cent of the average, the chosen tax rate is $33\frac{1}{3}$ per cent; if the median voter has earnings equal to 70 per cent of the average, the chosen tax rate is 50 per cent.

There are, however, well-known difficulties with the median voter model. Perhaps the most serious is that, once we consider decisions which have more than one dimension, the existence of a majority voting equilibrium becomes problematic. The BI/FT scheme is conveniently one-dimensional, in that once the tax rate is fixed, the basic income follows from the revenue constraint, but this would cease to be the case if we allowed for more than one rate of income tax. Foley (1967) considered the existence of a majority voting equilibrium with different tax structures, and showed that there is no such equilibrium where the class of tax schedules is unrestricted. The problem is even more acute with the social insurance/graduated tax alternative, which is inherently multidimensional. A graduated tax involves at least two marginal tax rates, as well as the tax threshold. The level of the social insurance benefit has to be determined.

Once we move to two or more dimensions, the conditions corresponding to single-peakedness become extremely restrictive, and a majority voting equilibrium may well not exist.

Cycling between different options becomes a distinct possibility. Consider the following example, where we have three packages:

A flat tax, medium level of SI
B graduated tax, high level of SI
C graduated tax, low level of SI

If the population consists of three equal-sized groups, the Rich, the Middle and the Poor, it is possible that

> The Rich prefer A to C, as they will pay less tax with the flat rate, even though the total revenue raised is more, and they prefer C to B as the tax rates are lower (and they get no benefit from the SI);
> The Middle prefer C to B on the grounds that the tax rates are lower (and they get no benefit from the SI), but rank B ahead of A because they pay less with the graduated tax (more of the cost falls on the Rich);
> The Poor rank the packages according to the levels of SI, preferring B to A to C.

It may then be verified that B defeats A in a straight vote (the Middle and the Poor being in favour), that C defeats B (the Rich and the Middle forming a majority), but that A defeats C (the Rich and the Poor forming a majority). None of the three packages can command a majority against the other two.

This means that we have to consider more carefully the structure of the political process. The setting of the agenda becomes critical. If the Middle group in the example can get the option A off the agenda, then they can assure that their preferred option is chosen. The existence of a majority voting outcome may be ensured by making further assumptions. Cukierman and Meltzer (1991) assume that there is a ranking of taxpayers independent of the tax policy, allowing them to analyse a two-parameter tax system (but without the SI feature of our example). Meltzer and Richard (1985) suppose that voters decide on single issues at a time. An equilibrium is then defined as a situation where a particular tax rate (say) commands a majority against all others, given the decisions on (say) the division of spending. This in effect limits the range of challenges which can be made to any potential majority voting equilibrium.

A particular form of agenda-setting is the design of political platforms by political parties. In a two-party system, the voter in the example may be presented only with a choice between B and C. A party seeking to build a coalition of the Rich and the Middle may support C, as being ranked first by one and second by the other; a party establishing a coalition of Middle and Poor may support B on the same grounds. This raises the question as to how parties form their political platforms. As modelled in the recent economics literature (for example, Alesina 1988 and Lindbeck and Weibull 1993), parties are concerned both with securing election and with pursuit of their ideological objectives. The existence of the latter means that there may be issues of credibility: a party may announce a platform of low taxes and then, after the election, pursue a policy of high taxes.

The voting model sees the electorate as decisive. Other theories see governments as at best constrained by the preferences of the electorate, and able to exercise considerable discretion. This discretion may reside with the legislature, with the executive, or with the administration. This may in turn lead to models of the interests of the government, as an independent actor. It may for example be argued, as by Brennan and Buchanan (1977 and 1978), that the power of the bureaucracy is such that the government should be modelled as a 'Leviathan' seeking to maximize its size. Or it may be that the government is seen as dominated by interest groups seeking to extract rent.

There is not scope in this book to examine all the variety of ideas which the public choice approach has produced. Instead, in the next section I consider one view of the political process which appears particularly applicable to the issue of tax design and which has close associations with Wicksell and Lindahl.

4.7 The Fiscal Constitution Model and Design of Taxation

One important development in the public choice framework has been that by Buchanan and his colleagues of the idea of a 'fiscal constitution'. According to this theory, Wicksell's idea of voluntary participation is applied to the constitutional stage of choice, when the rules of policy formation are determined. In his *Public Finance in Democratic Process*, Buchanan explains how

Under a democratic political order, individuals do more than choose in the market place and participate in collective choice under given institutions. Ultimately, at some 'constitutional' stage of decision, they must also select or choose the structural framework for choice itself; they must choose the institutions under which both day-to-day market choices and ordinary political choices are implemented. (1967: 214)

The broad features of fiscal *structure*, like whether there is a BI/FT system or a SI/GT system, then acquire the status of 'quasi-constitutionality' different from that of other changes in policy variables.

The case for treating issues of tax structure differently in this way has been argued by Brennan:

it is a notable feature of the tax system, and often of the process of tax reform, that they carry an aura of constitutionality. The basic system of tax tends to remain in place for long periods of time; root and branch 'reforms' are occasional affairs and are frequently conducted in a manner designed to insulate them from the influences of day-to-day politics. (1988: 46)

He goes on to refer to the setting up of special commissions or committees, whose style of operation is more 'judicial' than political, instancing the Carter Commission in Canada, the Asprey Taxation Reform Committee in Australia and the Meade Committee in the United Kingdom. The role of such bodies should not, however, be exaggerated: their recommendations are not invariably—or even perhaps usually—enacted, even when they were set up by the government (and the last of the committees instanced was not in fact an official body).

The constitutional stage of determining the structural rules is assumed to be separate from the day-to-day choices in the sense that people are supposed to be to a degree uncertain about the implications of different rules for their own interests: 'a given individual has no way of predicting just what proposals are likely to be presented to the group for choice [and] he has no way of predicting just where his own preferences would fall with regard to specific motions' (Buchanan 1967: 217). Institutions are to be chosen in a state of uncertainty, as in the choice of collective decision rules analysed by Buchanan

and Tullock in *The Calculus of Consent* (1962), or in the justification given by Harsanyi (1953) for utilitarianism, or in the
original position of Rawls (1971).

At the constitutional stage, people are assumed to be guided
by a degree of impersonality; they are assumed to act as if they
were behind a 'veil of ignorance' about their own interests. In
this context, Buchanan argues, people may vote for a progressive income tax even though they appreciate that they may
end up facing a high tax bill. As a result, 'Egalitarian aims,
explicitly avowed as ethical norms, need not be introduced to
'defend' the institution of progression' (1967: 237). At the same
time, he recognizes that people may be influenced by such
ethical norms. Real-world political debate is often couched in
terms of general principles of justice, or of notions of desert, or
of concern for individual liberty. It is in this way that I see my
earlier analysis as complementing the public choice approach.

What would be the implications of such a view of the political
process for the issue with which we are concerned? Suppose
that a constitutional agreement is the first stage in the process,
and that at the second stage decisions are made about the tax
rate and other parameters according to the regular day-to-day
political machinery. In other words, we have, as described in
Chapter 1:

Constitutional choice
    BI/FT   versus   SI/GT
Political machinery
    level of tax rate   level of tax rates
                             level of SI benefits

It is at this second stage that the public choice theories cited
in the previous section become relevant. Suppose for example
that the decisions at the second stage are made by majority
voting. This means that the first-stage choice between BI/FT
and SI/GT has to take account of the majority voting outcome.
We are not then choosing between the *optimal* level of the basic
income and the *optimal* SI/GT system. Rather we are choosing
between the basic income that would result from a majority
vote and the SI/GT that would result from voting. (It is here
that problems of existence may raise their head.)

This constitutional choice perspective may lead us to view

differently the choice of fiscal system. I do not know in which way the choice will be affected. It is possible for example that, even though an optimally chosen SI/GT would be preferable to the BI/FT on account of its greater number of parameters, the particular policy that would emerge from majority voting would actually be inferior to the BI/FT chosen by a majority. On the other hand, the reverse may be true. 'Targeted' SI may enjoy more electoral support, so that it provides a more effective redistributive device than the basic income. Even though the basic income might enjoy support at the first stage, the realities of electoral behaviour may be such that it would only be enacted at a very low level.

4.8 Concluding Comments

In this chapter, I have considered some of the non-welfarist principles which may guide the choice of government policy, particularly those concerned with individual freedom. We have seen that the relation between liberty and social welfare can take different forms. There may be a hierarchy of principles; there may be a higher-order maximand; there may be unavoidable conflicts of values.

Perhaps the most discussed view is that liberty and welfare maximization are in conflict, through the necessity to raise taxation, and that liberty has priority. In the context of redistribution via a basic income, or social insurance, this imposes an upper limit on the tax rates which may be levied. For some people, those favouring a minimal state, this limit may be zero. Constraints on redistribution may also arise on grounds of avoiding dependency on the state (although at the cost of increasing it on the family) and of desert. It is possible that the restrictions arising from these objectives, including individual freedom, may be less significant for categorical contributory social insurance than for the basic income. An alternative view is that the objectives may be reconciled rather than in conflict, pursuit of social welfare being complementary with the goal of effective liberty. In an affluent society where maximal liberty is potentially accessible to all, a basic income may be needed to ensure that effective liberty for all, and a conditional social insurance scheme may not provide the same guarantee.

This chapter has also considered public choice theory. Some may see this as a totally separate, and rival, approach. I have tried, however, to suggest that the constitutional model provides a role at the first stage for considerations of social welfare and justice, reconciling different points of departure.

5 A Richer Model of the Labour Market

5.1 Introduction

The theoretical model of labour supply used so far has provided a convenient laboratory within which to explore different approaches to the formation of public policy. For this purpose, the simplicity of the model has been an advantage. However, there can be little doubt that, in order to compare the realworld impact of the basic income scheme with that of the existing alternative of social insurance, a richer theoretical framework is necessary. A key element in the comparison is that the existing social security provisions are tied to specific contingencies such as unemployment or sickness, and we need therefore a model in which contingencies of this kind can arise. Unemployment may appear in the optimum taxation framework outlined earlier, in the sense of people choosing to work zero hours, but an adequate treatment needs to take account of such factors as efficiency wages, segmentation of the labour market, and involuntary unemployment.

The introduction of these considerations is particularly relevant to the *incidence* of the policy reform. In the simple optimum taxation analysis it was assumed that the factor prices (and, implicitly, the product prices) are unchanged by the introduction of the Basic Income/Flat Tax. There is assumed to be an infinitely elastic demand for labour of each quality at the specified wage rate. In contrast, the models of general equilibrium tax incidence of the type developed by Harberger (1962) tend to make simpler assumptions about the distribution of income, but to allow for changes in factor and product prices. They too are of the Arrow–Debreu type, with unemployment only appearing if labour is in excess supply at a zero wage rate, and what is needed is to extend these models to bring in other explanations of unemployment.

A richer framework is perhaps most relevant to the benefit side of the proposed reform but is also necessary on the financing side. One feature of the reform to which I have not yet paid much attention is that the social security payroll tax would be abolished and replaced by a general income tax. The payroll tax differs from the income tax in that it is levied on wage income and not on capital income. It may also differ in that part of the economy is typically not covered by the social security payroll tax: for example, part-time workers may not be liable for social security taxes even though they are, in principle, liable to the income tax.

This chapter makes a step in the direction of a richer model of the labour market, which allows for the possibility of un-employment. It is only a partial step. Many important con-siderations—such as uncertainty—remain outside the scope of the model. The comparison on the benefit side is limited to unemployment benefit. But it does take account of some of the institutional features of the latter, including the distinc-tion between unemployment insurance and unemployment assistance.

5.2 The Harberger Model of Tax Incidence

The natural starting-point for the general equilibrium theory of incidence is the model of Harberger (1962). His article on the incidence of the corporation income tax led to the widespread adoption by public finance economists of the two-good two-factor general equilibrium model. Two goods, denoted here by X and Y, are assumed to be produced by two sectors using two factors, capital and labour. The prices of goods, and the factor returns (the wage rate and the rate of return to capital) are determined perfectly competitively. Capital and labour are taken to be in fixed total supply, in quantities K and L respect-ively. What is determined in equilibrium is the allocation between the two sectors, and the associated levels of output of the two sectors, denoted by x and y. (For reviews of the contribution of the Harberger model, see, among others, Mieszkowski 1969, McLure 1975, and Kotlikoff and Summers 1987.)

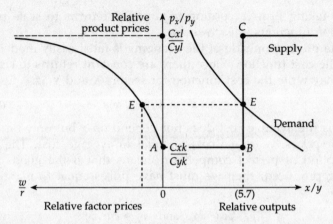

Fig. 5.1 General equilibrium with fixed coefficients (X sector labour-intensive)

The wide use of the Harberger model reflects the fact that it encompasses the essentials of an equilibrium model, while allowing a convenient representation in terms either of geometry (as in Johnson 1971) or the 'hat calculus' of Jones (1965 and 1971). The essentials are set out below. On the demand side, I simplify by assuming that all consumers have identical preferences and that the income elasticities of demand are equal to unity. This means that the relative demands for the two goods are independent of the distribution and level of income, depending only on the relative prices of the two goods, p_x/p_y. This relation is shown as a 'demand curve' in the right-hand segment of Figure 5.1. The assumptions about the demand side mean that neither a tax on all income, nor the payment of a basic income, affect the demand curve. Even if the basic income were financed from outside the country, people would spend it in the same proportions, so that the ratio of x to y demanded at any relative prices of the two goods, p_x/p_y, would be the same.

What does the 'supply curve' look like? Capital and labour are assumed to be in fixed total supply, but they are perfectly mobile between sectors. The wage is denoted by w and the rate of return by r. The output is produced by profit-maximizing

price-taking firms according to constant returns to scale production functions in each sector.

The production side of the economy is most easily modelled
via the cost function. Since there are constant returns to scale,
we may write the cost function for sectors X and Y as:

$$c_x(r, w) \, x \quad \text{and} \quad c_y(r, w)y \tag{5.1}$$

that is the average cost does not depend on x but only on the
factor prices. Marginal cost is equal to average cost. The assumption of perfect competition means that if the goods are
being produced, then we must have prices equal to marginal
costs:

$$p_x = c_x(r,w); \quad \text{and} \quad p_y = c_y(r,w) \tag{5.2}$$

From equations (5.2), we can see the relation between the
relative prices of the products and the factor prices. That is
p_x/p_y depends on r and w. Intuitively, the relation depends on
the relative importance of the factors in the production of the
two goods. If Y were to use almost entirely capital and X
almost entirely labour, then a rise in the ratio w/r would cause
the relative price of X to rise. If

$$X \text{ is labour-intensive relative to } Y \tag{5.3}$$

then we would find that p_x/p_y is an increasing function of w/r.
An example is shown in the left-hand quadrant of Figure 5.1,
with w/r on the horizontal axis (increasing as we move to the
left).

Price is one of the two important decisions that firms make
in this model. The other concerns the quantities of factors
used. Since the factor demands are obtained by differentiating
the cost function with respect to the factor prices, the quantity
of capital used in X is given by

$$c_{xk}(r, w)x \tag{5.4a}$$

where the subscript k denotes the derivative with respect to r,
and similarly the quantity of capital used in Y is given by

$$c_{yk}(r, w)y \tag{5.4b}$$

The demand for labour is obtained by differentiating with
respect to w. It may be noted that in the case of a fixed

coefficient production function, assumed below, the input requirements per unit of output do not depend on the factor prices.

Using (5.4), we can write the condition for equilibrium in the market for capital as:

$$c_{xk}x + c_{yk}y \leqslant K \qquad (5.5a)$$

and similarly the condition for equilibrium in the labour market is that

$$c_{xl}x + c_{yl}y \leqslant L \qquad (5.5b)$$

For an equilibrium, we either have to have equality, or inequality with the relevant factor price zero. So if labour were in excess supply, then the wage would have to be zero. In general we would expect the labour requirements to rise as w fell, so that we would have an interior equilibrium with labour supply and demand equal.

In order to ease the exposition, I now concentrate on the case of fixed coefficients of production: the terms c_{xk} etc. are constant. There is no choice of technique. The fact that there is no scope for varying the capital-labour ratio within each sector does not, however, mean that one factor must be in excess supply. The overall demand for the two factors depends on the relative outputs of the two sectors. Setting (5.5a) and (5.5b) to be equalities, and solving, we can see that if

$$\frac{c_{xk}}{c_{xl}} < \frac{K}{L} < \frac{c_{yk}}{c_{yl}} \qquad (5.6)$$

there is one pair of x and y which will give a full employment equilibrium. The ratio of x/y which ensures full employment is given by

$$\frac{x}{y} = \frac{c_{yk} - c_{yl}\dfrac{K}{L}}{c_{xl}\dfrac{K}{L} - c_{xk}} \qquad (5.7)$$

The right-hand inequality of (5.6) insures that the numerator is positive; the left-hand inequality insures that the denominator is positive. This ratio of x/y is shown on the horizontal axis in

the right hand-part of Figure 5.1, there being in the fixed
coefficient case no direct link between w/r and the output of
the two sectors.

There is no guarantee that a full employment equilibrium is
possible. The 'supply curve' in the fixed coefficient case in fact
consists of three segments. The first is the horizontal segment
AB where only the capital market is clearing, and the wage rate
is zero. The relative product prices are then simply the ratio of
the capital costs

$$\frac{r_y}{r_x} = \frac{c_{xk}}{c_{yk}} \tag{5.8a}$$

The second is the vertical segment BC where both factors are
fully employed, and the relative product prices are

$$\frac{r_x}{r_y} = \frac{c_{xl}w + c_{xk}r}{c_{yl}w + c_{yk}r} \tag{5.8b}$$

This is the form of the curve shown in the left-hand quadrant
of Figure 5.1. Finally, there is the horizontal segment right-
wards from C, where the relative product prices are determined by labour costs

$$\frac{r_x}{r_y} = \frac{c_{xl}}{c_{yl}} \tag{5.8c}$$

Equilibrium with full employment of both factors occurs where
the aggregate demand curve cuts the supply curve on the
vertical segment BC, as shown in Figure 5.1. The perfectly
competitive equilibrium is at E (indicated as such in both
quadrants).

5.3 The Incidence of the Social Security Tax

Under the basic income/flat tax proposal, the social security
payroll tax would be replaced by a proportional tax on all
income. The Harberger model may be used to analyse the
impact of this change in the method of financing income
transfers: the differential incidence of the social security tax
compared with the general income tax, which, under the

assumptions of the model described in the previous section, reduces all income proportionately.

General Payroll Tax

If the employer payroll tax is a *general factor tax*, falling on labour in all uses, then under the assumptions of the model the differential incidence is on labour. The effect of social insurance contributions is that, for any pre-tax wage w, the employee receives

$$w(1 - t_E) \tag{5.9}$$

where t_E is the employeE tax rate, and that the employer pays

$$\omega = w(1 + t_R) \tag{5.10}$$

where t_R is the employeR tax rate. If the analysis of Figure 5.1 is conducted in terms of ω, then it may be verified that nothing changes as the tax rates changes. It follows that the employee receives net of tax

$$\frac{\omega(1 - t_E)}{(1 + t_R)} \tag{5.11}$$

The payroll tax, whether charged on the employer or the employee, reduces the net wage.

On this basis, the switch in the method of financing shifts the burden from those with labour income to those with capital income, in that the payroll tax falls only on labour income and the income tax on all income. This conclusion would not, however, necessarily hold if the total factor supplies varied with the net factor return. Feldstein (1974) examines the case where capital continues to be in fixed supply, but labour is supplied according to the iso-elastic function studied in earlier chapters (a situation which may be regarded as corresponding to short-run incidence):

$$L = L_0[w(1 - t_E)]^\varepsilon \tag{5.12}$$

Considering an economy with a single sector, so that there are no changes in relative product prices, Feldstein shows that in the case of an infinitesimal tax (i.e. evaluating the derivative at

$t_E = 0$) the ratio of labour's net loss to the tax revenue collected is given by

$$\frac{1}{1 + (1 - \theta_l)(\varepsilon/\sigma)} \tag{5.13}$$

where θ_l is the share of wage costs in total costs of production (labour's factor share) and σ is the aggregate elasticity of substitution, assumed to be non-zero. This expression may be compared with the value of 1 which applies to taxation on capital income (assuming that capital is in fixed supply). The higher the elasticity of supply, and the smaller the elasticity of substitution, the more that labour shifts the burden on to incomes in general. If the labour supply were to approach being perfectly elastic (ε tend to infinity), then the loss to labour would tend to zero. To the extent that the burden of the payroll tax does not fall on labour income, the impact of the switch in financing is reduced.

If we return to a two-sector model, then the rise in the wage cost to the employer (where labour does not bear the full burden) has a differential impact on the two sectors, tending to raise the relative price of the labour intensive X sector. This might, however, be modified if the payroll tax were to be levied differentially on the two sectors, a possibility to which I now turn.

Partial Payroll Tax

There is a case for treating the social security payroll tax as a *partial factor tax*, falling on only one sector of the economy, so that there is a covered and an uncovered sector. Those employments not covered may include those in temporary work, those working less than a specified number of hours, those below a specified earnings threshold, and those in the shadow economy. Another interpretation is that of the uncovered sector as household production (see Boskin 1972 and 1975a, and Break 1974: 169). Or the social security scheme may be operated by trade unions, in which case there will be differential coverage, as analysed by Holmlund and Lundborg (1989).

In order to examine the question of the coverage of social

insurance, let us now suppose that the division of the economy into two sectors is no longer the corporate and non-corporate sectors considered by Harberger but the covered and uncovered sectors. This has been examined by Brittain (1972: 33–5) for the special case where the production functions are identical in the two sectors and of the Cobb–Douglas form, and where the demand functions are also Cobb–Douglas.

Here I retain the assumption of fixed coefficients of production. The partial factor tax does not therefore affect the choice of production technique. The equations for factor market clearing are unaffected. In terms of the diagrammatic analysis, there is no change in the ratio x/y consistent with full employment. The effect of the partial social security tax is to be found in the left-hand quadrant—see Figure 5.2. The impact depends on whether the covered sector is the labour-intensive sector (X) or the capital-intensive sector (Y). The reasons given earlier for incomplete coverage suggest that the latter is more likely to be the case, and this is assumed in Figure 5.2.

The condition for equality of net wages in the two sectors now requires that

$$\frac{\omega_y(1 - t_E)}{(1 + t_R)} = w_x \tag{5.14}$$

where the left-hand side is the gross payment by the employer in the covered sector, ω_y, reduced by the two types of tax. This can be rewritten as requiring that

$$\omega_y = \frac{1 + t_R}{1 - t_E} \cdot w_x \equiv T w_x \tag{5.15}$$

This may be substituted into the price equations to obtain the relation shown in the left-hand quadrant of Figure 5.2, where it may be noted that the variable on the horizontal left-hand axis is w_x/r.

The effect of the tax is to shift the price curve downwards, since the price of the Y product rises at all points except $w = 0$, where the tax has no impact. Since the equilibrium product prices do not change, the effect of the tax is to raise the equilibrium value of w_x/r, from the value indicated by E to E'. Put the other way, the abolition of the social security tax would have the effect of reducing the equilibrium value of the net

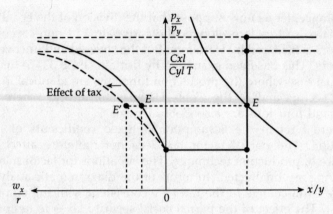

Fig. 5.2 Effect of partial payroll tax on Y sector

wage, relative to r. This may seem counter-intuitive, but the explanation is straightforward. In the absence of any substitution between capital and labour in production, a partial factor tax operates like an excise tax and 'hurts' the factor used intensively in its production. By assumption the covered sector is capital-intensive. If this were reversed, then so would be the conclusion.

In this simple general equilibrium model, the removal of social insurance contributions, whether employer or employee (in this model their impact is the same), would tend to benefit the factor of production used intensively in the sector of the economy covered by social insurance. Such a possible change in factor prices would need to be taken into account in the distributional analysis. At the same time, as with the general payroll tax, the conclusion would need to be modified if we were to change the assumptions of the model. If, for instance, there were substitutability between labour and capital in production in the covered sector, then this would tend to operate in the opposite direction from the excise effect just identified (where the covered sector is relatively capital-intensive). Firms previously subject to the payroll tax would find, with its abolition, that labour had become cheaper relative to capital and would choose a more labour-intensive technique. This in turn would tend to raise the net wage relative to r. The model needs, however, to be refined in other respects before we can draw definite conclusions.

5.4 A Dual Labour Market

In this section, I develop further the sectoral division of the economy by combining it with the notion of a dual labour market. The idea of labour market segmentation has a long history in institutional labour economics and has been popular among radical economists, but it has recently begun to attract mainstream attention.

The dual labour market formulation has been advanced by Doeringer and Piore (1971), who see the economy as having a favoured high-wage primary sector and a low-wage secondary sector. In the primary sector, there is stable employment, internal promotion possibilities, provision of training, and typically the work involves skill or the exercise of responsibility. In the secondary sector, jobs are typically unskilled, involve little training or prospect of promotion, and there is casual attachment between firms and workers. According to Bulow and Summers, 'A typical example of a primary-sector employer is a large manufacturing establishment, while small service firms such as fast food outlets typify the secondary sector' (1986: 380). This should be understood as a stylization. In reality a particular industrial sector may contain both primary and secondary jobs; none the less, the dual labour market model provides a sectoral distinction with an evident economic rationale, the implications of which seem worth pursuing. Moreover, the secondary sector has a number of features which mean that it is less likely to be covered by the payroll tax, including relatively short-term or casual employment, and illegal employment. In what follows this is represented in extreme form by assuming that the payroll tax falls only on the primary sector.

One of the aims of the recent literature is to seek to explain the persistence of a wage differential for otherwise identical workers, as a result of the characteristics of the two sectors. Particular weight has been given to the efficiency wage explanation. In the version developed by Shapiro and Stiglitz (1984),

Bowles (1985), Bulow and Summers (1986), and others, this is related to the costs of supervision in the two sectors. In the secondary sector, jobs are relatively easily supervised, whereas jobs in the primary sector require a degree of responsibility and initiative. Supervision is costly, and primary sector firms pay a wage premium in order to induce effort with only intermittent monitoring. If Y is the primary sector, and X the secondary sector, then a wage differential $w_y > w_x$ can persist in equilibrium. Suppose that the cost of effort is e, and that there is an exogenous probability q of being monitored. The primary sector worker is assumed to weigh the certainty of $(w_y - e)$ if he puts in effort against the probability $(1 - q)$ of w_y plus the probability q of being fired and earning $(w_x - e)$ in the secondary sector. (It is assumed for convenience that workers are risk-neutral and consider only income in a single period.) The wage premium necessary to just induce effort is (see MacLeod and Malcomson 1993, for further discussion of the contractual basis):

$$w_y = w_x + (e/q)(1 - q) \equiv w_x + \rho \qquad (5.16)$$

The premium ρ increases with the cost of effort and falls with the probability of being monitored.

In the dual labour market model there is the question of the ease of mobility between the sectors. A geographical interpretation of the Harberger model has been given by McLure (1969), where one of the two factors is not mobile between the sectors. In the case of labour, such frictions may be due to barriers to migration, as in the model of a developing dual economy of Harris and Todaro (1970). This model has been combined with that of efficiency wages (Stiglitz 1982) and has been applied to a developed country, where there are barriers to movement between the secondary and primary sectors and recruitment to the primary sector is from a pool of unemployed seeking jobs. As described by McDonald and Solow,

secondary employment may be regarded as a kind of stigma that bars access to the primary sector. To the extent that secondary workers are regarded by primary market employers as 'inferior' or 'unreliable', some gesture of separation from the secondary market may increase the chance of being offered a primary-sector job. (1985: 1124–5)

This leads to a queue of workers waiting for primary sector jobs, introducing into the model an equilibrium explanation of unemployment.

The consequences of these frictions for the analysis of tax incidence may be seen by modifying the earlier version of the Harberger model to allow for efficiency wages and for a queue of workers waiting for jobs in the primary sector. (Efficiency wages are introduced into the Harberger model by Agell and Lundborg (1992); the model here differs in emphasizing the primary/secondary distinction, as in van de Klundert (1988) and Atkinson (1988). The Harberger model has been modified to include search unemployment by Davidson, Martin, and Matusz 1987 and 1988.)

The probability of getting a job in the primary sector is the ratio, V/U, of the number of vacancies to the number of unemployed competing for them, where V is assumed to be less than U. Workers can move freely between unemployment and secondary sector employment. The wage paid by the latter, w_x, is then compared with the expected value of a wage, w_y, in the primary sector with probability V/U or continued unemployment with probability $(1 - V/U)$. For there to be indifference between secondary employment and unemployment, this means that

$$w_x = (V/U)w_y + (1 - V/U)e \qquad (5.17)$$

where e is the value of the effort expended at work and hence the net benefit when unemployed (no account is taken at this point of unemployment insurance).

It is assumed that a randomly selected fraction g of those with jobs in the primary sector are made redundant for exogenous reasons, and that an equal number of vacancies are created, so that the rate of success is

$$V/U = \frac{gL_y}{L - L_x - L_y} \qquad (5.18)$$

where L_x, L_y denote employment in the X and Y sectors, respectively, and the denominator in (5.18) is the number of unemployed workers.

Using equation (5.16) to eliminate w_y, the resulting goods price relationship is shown in the left-hand upper quadrant of

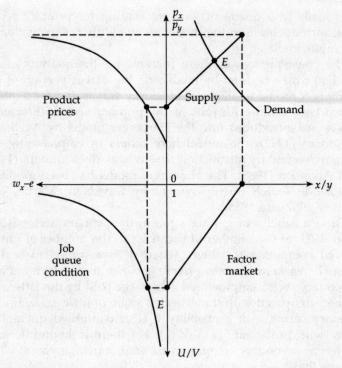

Fig. 5.3 General equilibrium in dual labour market model with queue unemployment

Figure 5.3, where the horizontal axis measures $(w_x - e)$, the profit rate r being taken as the numeraire ($r = 1$). I continue to assume that there are fixed coefficients of production, so that the price equations are

$$p_x = c_{xl}w_x + c_{xk}; \quad p_y = c_{yl}(w_x + \rho) + c_{yk} \qquad (5.19)$$

The ratio p_x/p_y forms a curve which starts at $c_{xk}/(c_{yk} + c_{yl}\rho)$ and tends as w_x tends to infinity to c_{xl}/c_{yl}. The assumption about capital-intensity means that it slopes up to the left.

The factor market equations are

$$c_{xl}x + c_{yl}y(1 + gU/V) = L \quad \text{and} \quad c_{xk}x + c_{yk}y = K \qquad (5.20)$$

where the queue of unemployed has been included in the second term of the first equation. If it is assumed that

$$\frac{c_{xk}}{c_{xl}} < \frac{K}{L} < \frac{c_{yk}}{c_{yl}}/[1 + g(U/V)] \tag{5.21}$$

for a range of U/V greater than 1, then we can solve for x/y in terms of U/V:

$$\frac{x}{y} = \frac{Lc_{yk} - Kc_{yl}[1 + g(U/V)]}{Kc_{xl} - Lc_{xk}} \tag{5.22}$$

As shown in the right-hand lower quadrant of Figure 5.3, the relation gives a straight line sloping down to the left and reaching the vertical axis where the second inequality in (5.21) fails to hold.

The final relationship is that between U/V and w_x. Substituting again from equation (5.16), we can show this relation in the bottom left-hand quadrant of Figure 5.3:

$$w_x - e = \frac{\rho}{(U/V) - 1} \tag{5.23}$$

This gives a rectangular hyperbola.

From this model with frictional unemployment and efficiency wages, we can see the impact of a payroll tax on the covered (Y) sector. Again the assumption of fixed coefficients means that the factor mix is unaffected. The queue condition is also unaffected. The only relationship which is shifted is that for the product prices in the left-hand upper quadrant. The after-tax equilibrium may be seen from Figure 5.4 to shift production towards the uncovered sector (from E to E'), with a rise in the wage rate in both sectors (the wage premium is unaffected). The new findings concern the equilibrium level of unemployment. The effect of the tax is to reduce U/V and to reduce employment in the Y sector (and hence V). So, with the assumptions made, the use of the payroll tax in place of a general income tax would reduce unemployment.

Conversely, the replacement of the social security tax by a general income tax would raise frictional unemployment. This is not altogether surprising. Social insurance was introduced in order to provide for the unemployment (and other contingencies) associated with the modern employment relationship in the industrial sector (Atkinson 1991*b*). The levying of the payroll tax in itself tended to reduce employment in that sector

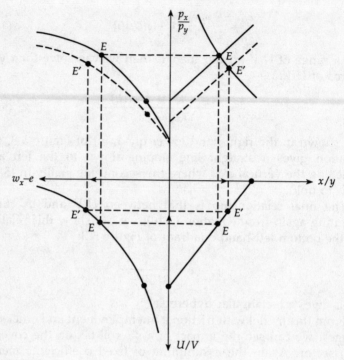

Fig. 5.4 Effect of payroll tax on primary (Y) sector in dual labour market model

(although this may have been offset by the value of the benefits to which it gave entitlement). A general income support system, financed by general taxation, would not have these sectoral implications.

Such a finding is in part a product of the assumptions made, and alternative assumptions could lead to a reversal of the result. This is not, however, a criticism of the approach. We should not expect to be able to reach strong conclusions without introducing specific features of the economy.

5.5 Basic Income in Place of Unemployment Benefit

An important feature of the basic income proposal is that it would replace a benefit conditional on employment status by one paid irrespective of whether the recipient is employed or unemployed. The basic income is neutral with respect to the decision whether to work in the X sector or to join the queue for jobs in the Y sector, since the basic income is paid to the unemployed and employed alike. It is equally neutral with respect to the decision whether or not to put in effort, since the same amount is paid.

How would the replacement of unemployment benefit by a basic income affect the working of the labour market? This depends on the form of unemployment benefit. In much of the literature on unemployment benefit, it is assumed that the benefit operates just like a wage for the unemployed: for example, 'the wage when working is w, and is b when not working' (Oswald 1986: 369). If that is the way in which unemployment benefit works, then its effect is readily seen. We have to add the amount of benefit, I, to the value of e in equation (5.17):

$$w_x = (V/U)w_y + (1 - V/U)(e + I) \qquad (5.24)$$

The wage premium is unaffected, so substituting from (5.16), we obtain

$$w_x - e = I + \frac{\rho}{(U/V) - 1} \qquad (5.25)$$

As shown in Figure 5.5, the introduction of I shifts the curve in the left-hand lower quadrant to the left by a constant amount, and the 'supply curve' shifts upward. At the new equilibrium, the relative price of x rises, and its relative output falls. The wage rate, w_x, rises, but by less than the amount of the benefit, so that the 'replacement rate' rises. The level of U/V rises, and with it the level of unemployment.

Putting these results in reverse, the introduction of a basic income would be predicted to reduce unemployment and to reduce wage levels. This does, however, depend on unemployment benefit operating like a wage when not working. In fact, if one looks at *unemployment insurance* (UI), then we have to take account of the following institutional features:

(a) the benefit is refused, or there is a period of disqualification, where the claimant has quit employment voluntarily or has been dismissed for industrial misconduct,

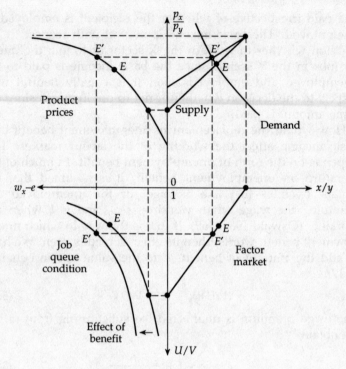

Fig. 5.5 Effect of unemployment benefit in dual labour market model

(b) entitlement to UI depends on the past record of insured employment, typically requiring a minimum earnings level for eligibility and a minimum contribution period,

(c) continued receipt of benefit is conditional on the recipient making demonstrable efforts to search for new employment, on being available for employment, and on accepting suitable job offers,

(d) there is limited duration of entitlement, after which UI benefit ceases to be paid.

As a result of these conditions, there may be a sizeable proportion of the unemployed who do not receive UI benefit. There are those who have been refused benefit, or disqualified for a period, on grounds of voluntary quitting, dismissal for industrial misconduct, for failing to carry out job search, or for refusing suitable job offers. There are those who do not satisfy the contribution conditions: for example new entrants to the labour force may not be eligible. There are those who have received UI earlier in their unemployment spell but whose entitlement is now exhausted.

In listing these features, I have referred explicitly to unemployment insurance, and it is important to distinguish this from *unemployment assistance* (UA). In some countries, UA is closer to the hypothetical 'wage when not working' in that there may be no contribution conditions, and that it may be paid for an unlimited duration. However, people may be disqualified from UA in the case of voluntary quitting or dismissal for industrial misconduct; and benefit may be withdrawn if they are not considered to be actively seeking employment or if they refuse suitable job offers.

These institutional features modify the conclusions drawn with respect to the impact of unemployment benefit. If unemployment insurance applies only to the covered sector, and is paid only in the event of job terminations unrelated to misconduct, then the benefit provided to workers by the existence of this insurance is reflected in the wages paid (Atkinson 1992). UI reduces the equilibrium level of wages paid in the covered sector. According to such an analysis, the replacement of UI by a basic income may be expected to make primary sector employment less attractive, putting upward pressure on wages in that sector. The number of vacancies in the primary sector per unemployed worker is reduced. There is a shift towards secondary sector employment; in effect a transfer from 'good jobs' to 'bad jobs'.

5.6 Concluding Comment

The model described in this chapter makes a step towards incorporating into the Harberger framework some of the recent developments in labour economics. At the same time, it has evident limitations. The explanation of unemployment in equilibrium terms does not mean that it may not arise as a disequilibrium phenomenon. Where markets do not clear, agents are rationed with regard to factor supplies and commodity demands. The modification of general equilibrium tax incidence to this type of situation has been examined by Dixit (1976) and Atkinson and Stiglitz (1980: 222–5), but it is intrinsically difficult.

6   Tax-Benefit Models

6.1 Introduction

Models based on representative samples of the population are now widely used in the analysis of tax and social security systems, and they have played a central role in discussions of possible reforms. Although some of these models now incorporate behavioural responses in terms of changes in labour supply or other decisions, an important role is played by models which are purely *arithmetical*. It was these models, and particularly the model TAXMOD (now called POLIMOD) developed by Holly Sutherland and myself (Atkinson and Sutherland 1988) as part of the ESRC Research Programme at the LSE, that the present chapter is concerned.

The TAXMOD model is in many respects like those employed in ministries of finance and treasury departments around the world. It makes use of data on the circumstances of a representative sample of individual families (obtained in our case from the regular household budget survey) to calculate the impact on net incomes of the current tax/benefit system, and compares it with that of the policy change. Models of this type have been widely used in government to examine the effect of changes in tax rates and allowances, or the impact of changing social security benefits, or of reforms that affect both taxation and social security.

What is different about our model is the emphasis we have placed on *accessibility*. A major aim of our research has been to bring this kind of model within the reach of those outside government. It is not locked in a security-conscious government department, nor is it the exclusive property of one particular research institute. The model is available to anyone who requests it, at marginal cost (in 1989 this was £75), and, just as important, it is written with the user in mind. The user is not required to have any computing expertise, only to know how to switch the machine on. The program is menu-driven, and contains information to prompt the user at each stage.

In this chapter, I begin by explaining why data on individual families and individuals is necessary in order to explore the quantitative implications of the basic income/flat tax reform. While aggregate calculations may be possible for the pure basic income scheme, involving the total abolition of all existing social security benefits, they cannot be used to calculate the impact of a partial basic income—which is the scheme most likely to enjoy political support. In Section 6.3, I describe two versions of the partial basic income.

6.2 Aggregate Arithmetic of a Full Basic Income

In principle the arithmetic of a basic income scheme is simple, and it is tempting to reach for the national income accounts (in the UK the Blue Book) and design a scheme without moving from one's armchair. The total amount of basic income that can be afforded is

> the tax rate times the tax base

minus

> existing revenue from income tax and employee National Insurance Contributions (NIC)

plus

> the cost of the present social security benefits which would be abolished.

From the 1987 Blue Book (Central Statistical Office 1987), we see that total household income from employment, self-employment, occupational pensions, and investments in 1986 was £253 billion and that £57 billion was paid in income tax and NIC. The present benefits cost £40 billion.

The stage is then set to calculate the basic incomes payable with different tax rates. If children aged 0–15 are treated as equivalent to two-thirds of an adult, then the number of equivalent adults in the UK is approximately 53 million. The basic income that could therefore be afforded with a tax rate of

34 per cent (i.e. taking the 1988/9 basic rate of income tax plus standard rate NIC) is

$$£ [0.34 \times 253 - 57 + 40] \times 1000/53/52 = £25 \text{ per week}$$

Put another way, the basic income would cost £69 billion.

A married man earning £200 a week (approximately the average at that time for male full-time workers) would be in the following situation:

	ACTUAL 1986/7	with BASIC INCOME
income tax/NIC	£55.62	£68.00
basic income	0	£50.00

He and his family appear to gain by over £37 a week. For a single man on the same earnings the position would be

	ACTUAL 1986/7	with BASIC INCOME
income tax/NIC	£62.98	£68.00
basic income	0	£25.00

He gains by nearly £20 a week.

There are two major difficulties with the simple arithmetic and these hypothetical examples of the impact of the basic income. The first is that the tax base is assumed to be equal to total personal income as measured in the Blue Book, whereas in practice this is far too optimistic. It includes, for example, an estimate of black economy earnings and untaxed income in kind which would be equally likely to escape under the basic income scheme; national accounts figures for self-employment income relate to currently accruing income, whereas tax liabilities arise on profits in a previous accounting year; the item for occupational pensions in the national accounts includes the refund of contributions and other items not subject to tax; and so on. A detailed investigation for 1982/3 (Atkinson 1989) suggested that the tax base was some 12 per cent lower, which would give £220 billion in 1986, with a resulting basic income of £21 per person. The total cost of the basic incomes would be £58 billion.

Even with more realistic figures for tax base, we still get a very favourable picture in the cases outlined above. The family of a man on average earnings gains nearly £30; and the single taxpayer gains £16. The second problem, however, is that such hypothetical examples are of essence selective, ignoring many of the features relevant to calculating a person's tax-benefit position. It is easy to think of situations where the basic income would involve a loss of income. Most importantly, those people without earnings would be likely to lose from the introduction of a basic income at this level. The long-term Supplementary Benefit scale rates in force in the first half of 1986 were £37.50 for a single person and £60.00 for a couple (the rates were increased on 28 July 1986). On top of this, householders would have been eligible for housing benefit.

The level of basic income needed to replace both Supplementary Benefit and housing benefit would be more than double the £21 figure. Parker (1989) takes a figure for 1985/6 of £60 a week for adults, with rates for children between £20 and £44. These could only be financed with a tax rate considerably higher than 34 per cent: Parker gives a range of estimates of the necessary tax rate of 68–86 per cent. The political opposition to tax rates at this kind of level has led in turn to proposals for a *partial basic income*, particularly by Rhys Williams and Parker (see Parker 1989), which would go part—but not all—of the way towards replacing current social insurance. The aim is to achieve a significant part of the objectives of the full basic income, without involving such a high tax rate.

One version of such a partial basic income in Britain could be achieved by replacing the present income tax allowances by refundable tax credits, which would provide the embryo of a basic income. The amount involved would be relatively small, but it represents a starting-point. If, moreover, the flat tax were introduced by taking the higher of the two rates in the UK, rather than the lower, that is levelling up to 40 per cent rather than levelling down to 25 per cent, coupled with some broadening of the tax base, then the result would be a quite substantial basic income. While still not enough to permit social security benefits to be completely abolished, it would represent a sizeable step in that direction.

Such a partial basic income cannot, however, be analysed on the basis of 'back of the envelope' calculations. Both the cost, and the effectiveness, can only be assessed by examining the impact on individual taxpayers. For example, the extent to which the partial basic income would float families off dependence on means-tested benefits depends on the individual circumstances of the family.

6.3 A Partial Basic Income

The partial basic income scheme examined here in effect 'cashes out' the personal income tax allowances, such as the single allowance, the married man's allowance, the wife's earned income allowance, and the allowance for single parents. Similarly, the basic income envisages that tax expenditures would be phased out and as a step towards this the partial scheme restricts the reliefs for mortgage interest and employee superannuation contributions to the basic rate of tax. The resulting extra revenue from these changes on the tax side is used to introduce basic incomes of £10 per person aged 16 or over. For those aged 16 or 17 in receipt of child benefit, this is made up of £7.25 child benefit plus £2.75 basic income, the distinction being important since child benefit does not enter the calculation of entitlement to family credit. All figures relate to October 1988, representing the fiscal year 1988/9. National Insurance and other benefits remain in place, but are reduced by the amount of the basic income, so that there is a switch in the type of benefit even where the cash amount is unchanged.

Such a partial basic income may be seen either as a compromise solution or as the first stage along the route to a full basic income. The latter takes account of the important consideration that, in terms of practical policy-making, what is relevant is not just the destination of reform but the process of transition by which such a full scheme could be approached. Because of its history—the scheme having first been discussed in wartime—discussions of a basic income have tended to assume that it could be introduced in a green field site. In fact, as the experience of the April 1988 social security changes has amply demonstrated, any reform needs to be planned carefully as a process of transition from the existing situation. The government cannot simply stop paying benefits for an interim period while the new provisions are implemented; no less can it cease collecting taxes. One has to get from here to there.

In what follows, the results of two versions of the partial

basic income are presented. The first (Scheme A) retains the basic rate of tax (25 per cent) in force in 1988/9 and pays a basic income of £10 a week, whereas the second (Scheme B) is more redistributive, taking the flat tax rate equal to the higher rate (40 per cent) and paying a substantially higher basic income (£35.60) a week. The schemes also differ in the following features:

Scheme A

  (a) allows a disregard of the first £16.60 of earnings per week,

  (b) income tax relief for mortgage interest and superannuation contributions limited to 25 per cent tax rate,

  (c) National Insurance benefits reduced by amount of basic income,

  (d) basic element (up to £31.15) of National Insurance benefits not subject to income tax,

  (e) invalidity benefit treated for tax purposes in same way as other National Insurance benefits,

  (f) wife's National Insurance pension received via derived rights treated as her own income for tax purposes.

  (g) retains the age allowance under the income tax, but this would be reduced to £1,040 with an income limit of £8,460.

Scheme B

  (a) income tax relief for mortgage interest abolished,

  (b) age allowances abolished,

  (c) composite rate tax on interest income set at 40 per cent,

  (d) child basic incomes set at £12 for those aged 15 and under, and £20 for those aged 16 and over,

  (e) National insurance benefits reduced by £17.80 per adult, but these remain taxable.

6.4 Using TAXMOD to Analyse the Impact of the Partial Basic Income

In the analysis that follows, we make use of the TAXMOD model to examine the implications of the partial basic income approach. (For further information about the model, see the book edited by Atkinson and Sutherland (1988), which includes contributions by the Institute for Fiscal Studies and other researchers in the field.)

TAXMOD is a micro-computer tax-benefit model that calculates the taxes and benefits of individual families which are then grossed up to be representative of the total population. The calculations are based on the information contained in the Family Expenditure Survey (FES) about income and family circumstances. The FES is a continuous survey of households carried out by the government and used for many purposes, including the collection of budget information necessary to obtain weights to be used in the construction of the retail prices index. The survey provides a rich source of data for the construction of tax-benefit models, although it has to be remembered that it was not designed primarily for this purpose and that in modelling taxes and benefits a number of assumptions have to be made (discussed further below).

The main aim of the model is to allow the user to examine the implications of policy changes, as you can see from the following menu:

MENU You may change:
1. Child benefit and Family Credit
2. National Insurance contributions
3. Income tax
4. NI retirement pension and widows benefits
5. Unemployment benefit, YTS and JTS
6. Sickness benefit, invalidity and maternity benefits
7. Housing benefit
8. Income support
9. Introduce new benefit

The changes which may be made are, of course, limited to those included in the program, but under each of these headings there is a wide range of options (contained in sub-menus).

The partial basic income scheme may be introduced into TAXMOD using the income tax and new benefit routines:

3. Income tax
9. Introduce new benefit

The tax treatment under the proposed partial basic income is essentially independent. Each person receives a basic income regardless of the income or other circumstances of anyone they are living with and their tax bill is equally unaffected. The income tax would become independent in a true sense. One-earner couples gain from the partial basic income, the amount having been set under Scheme A such that the basic income is worth 30p a week more than the value of the married man's allowance to a basic rate taxpayer. (For higher-rate taxpayers, there will be a loss.) On the other hand, it has the consequence that all earnings would become taxable from the first £1. The present administrative machinery may not be capable of doing this—it would mean that all small earnings should in theory be taxed at source. It is also the case that on the benefit side there is typically an earnings disregard for small amounts. For these reasons, version A of the partial basic income includes a disregard for earned income so that the first £16.60 of earnings are not taxed. This would be like a reduced personal allowance available to all workers. The effect of this is to provide a positive net gain to couples with one earner and to allow single earners to be net gainers. It is still, however, the case that two-earner couples are net losers.

This basic income is intended to replace in part existing social security benefits, so that these benefits are at the same time reduced. Under scheme A they are reduced by the amount of the basic income (£10); under scheme B, where the national insurance benefits remain taxable, the reduction is less than the increase in the basic income (since recipients would lose from the abolition of the income tax allowances). The changes in national insurance benefit are introduced in TAXMOD via the menu:

6. Sickness benefit, invalidity and maternity benefits

Further, we assume that the wife's pension is treated as her own income, using:

4. NI retirement pension and widows benefits.

The parameters of the partial basic income scheme described above have been chosen to secure revenue neutrality. This is indeed the first way in which TAXMOD may be used. One of the virtues of having the analysis accessible is that one can iterate; and this is what we have done to find a revenue-neutral version of scheme. Revenue neutrality has been secured in the case of Scheme A by varying the earned income disregard (arriving at a figure of £16.60); in the case of scheme B it has been reached by varying the amount of the basic income. It is this calculation that is done in the first stage of TAXMOD. The revenue figures are, however, built up from the calculations for individual families. Each number flashing on the screen corresponds to a family—the calculation taking a fifth of a second on an Apricot Xen 386 machine (state of the art in 1989).

The revenue calculation may be illustrated with respect to Scheme A. All figures relate to October 1988 (representing the fiscal year 1988/9), so that they are after the 1988 Budget and the April 1988 social security changes.

	Cost in £ billions per year in 1988/9		
	Difference	Current	Policy change
Income tax	−43	−58	−15
Basic incomes	0	22	+22
NI benefits	24	18	− 6
Income-tested benefits	9	8	− 1

The figures show a £22 billion expenditure on the basic incomes, with the cost being offset by the reductions in pensions and other NI benefits and by the large increase in income tax revenue, together with some saving from people being floated off means-tested benefits.

6.5 Impact on Individual Taxpayers: Scheme A

The second main use of TAXMOD is to investigate the extent of redistribution between individual families entailed by a partial basic income. In this section we consider Scheme A. Since the scheme is revenue neutral, there must be losers. Are they all higher rate taxpayers (for whom the loss of the tax allowance is not outweighed by the basic income) or two-earner couples or those with mortgages? The answers may lead to a revision of the scheme, and there may be a further round of iteration between proposals and results. Once one has seen who gains and loses from a particular scheme, it may become obvious how it could be strengthened.

For a sizeable proportion of families, the introduction of the basic income would be exactly offset by the reduction in existing social security benefits. This applies to a quarter of all families. For the remainder, there would be a net gain or a net loss, with the overall zero net cost being the result of pluses and minuses cancelling out. Table 6.1 gives the average gain or loss by income ranges. This shows a sizeable average loss for the top group, reflecting the loss to higher rate taxpayers, but on average a net gain for all other groups, with this being particularly marked for the bottom group (see Figure 6.1).

This suggests that a large majority of the three-quarters affected by the introduction of the partial basic income would be gainers; however, averages can be misleading, as is illustrated by Table 6.2, which shows for each of the ranges in Table 6.1

Table 6.1 Effect of partial basic income (Scheme A) by ranges of net income

Upper end of range £/week	Before change		After change		Average gain £/week
	% in range	Cumulative %	% in range	Cumulative %	
50	11.5	11.5	11.4	11.4	2.32
75	14.2	25.7	14.0	25.4	0.70
100	12.4	38.1	12.6	37.9	0.81
125	10.3	48.4	10.4	48.3	0.40
150	9.2	57.5	9.0	57.3	0.43
175	7.3	64.9	7.6	64.9	0.50
200	7.3	72.2	7.2	72.0	0.75
225	5.8	77.9	5.9	77.9	0.20
250	4.8	82.7	4.9	82.8	0.06
—	17.3	100.0	17.2	100.0	−3.81

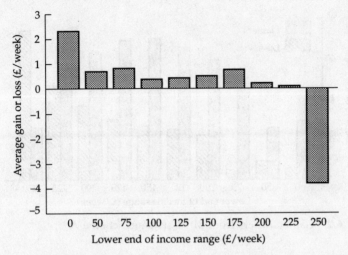

Fig. 6.1 Average gain from BI/FT scheme: Scheme A

Table 6.2 Effect of partial basic income (Scheme A): percentage with gains and losses

Range[a]	Absolute changes £/week						
	−15	−15/−5	−5/0	No change	0/5	5/15	15
1	0.1	2.9	2.6	65.9	6.2	19.4	2.9
2	—[b]	1.0	8.1	65.4	19.9	5.2	0.4
3	—	2.1	10.1	40.3	43.9	3.1	0.5
4	—	5.3	16.8	18.8	57.8	1.3	—
5	0.5	8.4	15.5	10.0	63.9	1.6	0.1
6	2.0	9.6	14.5	4.3	68.5	0.9	0.2
7	0.9	8.9	19.6	1.3	66.4	2.9	—
8	1.0	7.9	27.5	1.0	59.5	3.1	—
9	1.2	2.6	43.0	—	49.4	3.7	0.3
10	8.6	15.5	49.9	0.6	22.9	2.1	0.4
Overall	1.9	6.7	20.6	25.3	40.4	4.6	0.5

[a] The range refers to the row in Table 6.1.
[b] Blank entries are zero.

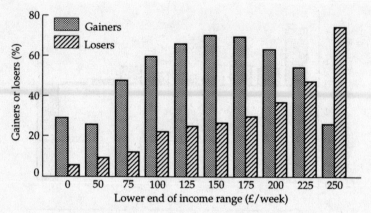

Fig. 6.2 Gainers/losers from BI/FT scheme: Scheme A

the distribution by range of gain or loss. Within all groups there are gainers and losers, depending on the precise situation of the different families concerned (see Figure 6.2). In the bottom group there are less than 30 per cent who are actual gainers; about two-thirds are unaffected by the reform (because of the offsetting of the basic income against NI benefits); and 6 per cent are net losers. Nor do those at the top necessarily lose. In the top group there are a quarter who are net gainers, including some who gain more than £5 a week. It is not even true that most losers are at the top. A fifth of all losers are in the bottom half of the distribution. This underlines the fact that it may be unhelpful to think about social security reforms in terms of a 'break-even' point below which people gain and above which people lose (or vice versa). Gains and losses depend very much on individual circumstances.

As Table 6.2 suggests, the introduction of a partial basic income would not in fact have very large effects on the distribution. Certainly the impact would be much less dramatic than that of a pure basic income. Table 6.3 shows the distribution of gains and losses by size. About 4 per cent lose more than £10 a week and about the same percentage gain more than £10 a week. In Section 6.6, I examine the more redistributive partial basic income with a 40 per cent tax rate.

Table 6.3 Effect of partial basic income (Scheme A): distribution of gains and losses

Change in net income (upper end of range) £/week	%	Cumulative %
−10	3.7	3.7
−8	1.6	5.2
−6	1.2	6.5
−4	2.7	9.1
−2	14.9	24.0
zero	5.1	29.1
no change	25.3	54.4
2	26.9	81.3
4	2.6	83.9
6	11.3	95.2
8	1.0	96.2
10	0.6	96.7
—	3.3	100.0

So far, we have looked at the impact on net incomes. The effects on the marginal tax rates are shown in Tables 6.4 and 6.5. Table 6.4 gives the marginal rate on £1 additional earnings by the family head, defined conventionally to be the husband in the case of a couple. Most people are in the 30–40 per cent range, where the marginal rate is 25 per cent basic rate income tax plus NIC; and the average marginal rate is about 33 per cent. The introduction of the partial basic income would not lead to major changes as far as the family head is concerned. A certain number are pushed into the higher rate band by the replacement of personal allowances by basic incomes and by the mortgage interest and superannuation contribution changes. The number in the poverty trap is slightly reduced, with the number of families receiving family credit reduced only by about one-seventh.

Turning to the marginal tax rate for the wife, we would expect this to go up since the amount of tax-free earnings has been reduced. On the other hand, there is the countervailing factor that independent taxation means that some wives no

Table 6.4 Effect of partial basic income (Scheme A): marginal tax rates for family head[a]

Range of marginal tax rate[b]	Before change		After change	
(upper end) (%)	%	Cumulative %	%	Cumulative %
10	3.0	3.0	2.1	2.1
20	—[c]	3.0	—	2.1
30	17.3	20.3	15.9	17.9
40	72.0	92.3	72.3	90.3
50	5.5	97.9	7.8	98.1
60	—	97.9	—	98.1
70	—	97.9	—	98.1
—	2.1	100.0	1.9	100.0
Average marginal tax rate		32.7		33.2
% with increased marginal tax rates			5.1	
% with decreased marginal tax rates			2.0	

[a] The results relate to families where the head is in paid employment.
[b] Calculated for £1 increase in the earnings of the family head.
[c] Blank entries are less than 0.1%.

longer face higher rates of tax on account of their husband's earnings. In order to assess the quantitative significance of these two considerations, we need a model like TAXMOD. From the results, the first of these factors seems to be much stronger, with an increase in the marginal rate for nearly 30 per cent. The average marginal rate for all wives does indeed rise by 5 percentage points.

These results will doubtless raise questions in the mind of the reader. For example, who are the losers in the bottom group and can this be avoided? How far does the variation in gain or loss by income range reflect the differing numbers of single and married people in the different ranges? What about bread-winner wives? How are gains and losses related to the receipt of current income-tested benefits? One of the attractions of the micro-technology is that the user can choose to explore

Table 6.5 Effect of partial basic income (Scheme A): marginal tax rates for wife[a]

Range of marginal tax rate[b] (upper end) (%)	Before change		After change	
	%	Cumulative %	%	Cumulative %
10	30.9	30.9	6.1	6.1
20	0.4	31.3	0.4	6.5
30	27.4	58.7	53.3	59.8
40	33.8	92.5	36.5	96.3
50	4.3	96.8	0.8	97.1
60	0.3	97.1	—[c]	97.1
70	—	97.1	—	97.2
—	2.9	100.0	2.8	100.0
Average marginal tax rate		27.0		32.2
% with increased marginal tax rates			28.6	
%. with decreased marginal tax rates			4.8	

[a] The results relate to those families where there is a wife in paid employment.
[b] Calculated for £1 increase in the earnings of the wife.
[c] Blank entries are less than 0.1%.

aspects which look interesting in a particular application. The production of further results can be left at the choice of the user. It is not like a book where there is only a restricted range of options. If the user wants to look at the figures a different way, then—providing the programming is sufficiently flexible—this can be chosen from the menu. TAXMOD allows the user to vary, for example, the ranges in Tables 6.1 and 6.2. It allows the user to choose from a number of other tables, including the construction of Lorenz curves, as is shown in the following menu:

1. Distribution of gains and losses by characteristics
2. Characteristics: gainers and losers

3. Distribution of changes in marginal tax rates by characteristics
4. List cases of large gains and losses
5. List cases where large changes in marginal tax rates
6. Lorenz curves
7. Incomes relative to poverty line
8. Hypothetical families

6.6 Impact of Partial Basic Income: More Redistributive Scheme B

Scheme A is designed maintaining a number of the parameters of the present system, notably the basic tax rate, and its redistributional impact is therefore limited. In this section, I examine Scheme B, which is more redistributive, with a substantially higher basic income financed by a tax rate of 40 per cent. This gives some flavour of the variation that can be achieved by changes in the parameters.

The wider redistribution will affect people in different income ranges, with those on low incomes typically making significant gains from the introduction of the basic income and those from average income upwards facing higher tax bills. But there will also be redistribution in other dimensions. It will affect single people differently from couples, in view of the independence of basic incomes, compared with the married couple's tax allowance. The scheme will differentially affect those with children and those without.

In considering this more redistributive scheme, we have therefore to pay closer attention to the treatment of families of different composition. In Tables 6.1 and 6.2, the income ranges refer to the total income of the family, irrespective of its size. This absence of adjustment for family composition is characteristic of the treatment of income distribution in the UK official statistics (until the introduction of the Households Below Average Income series), as in the Blue Book series (see Atkinson and Micklewright 1992, Statistical Appendix). But there are good arguments for considering a measure of income adjusted for family composition.

In Tables 6.6 and 6.7, families are classified by net *equivalent*

Table 6.6 Gains and losses from partial basic income (Scheme B) by range of equivalent net income

Ranges of equivalent income, upper end (£)	Before change		After change		Average gain £ per week
	%	Cumul.	%	Cumul.	
43.25	10.0	10.0	5.48	5.48	18.95
55.15	10.0	20.0	8.36	13.84	11.01
65.80	10.0	30.0	10.12	23.95	10.31
78.05	10.0	40.0	10.07	34.02	10.78
93.00	10.0	50.0	11.62	45.64	10.98
109.85	10.0	60.0	12.52	58.17	5.74
130.80	10.0	70.0	13.20	71.37	−0.61
159.90	10.0	80.0	12.65	84.02	−8.77
204.70	10.0	90.0	9.15	93.17	−19.59
—	10.0	100.0	6.83	100.00	−39.15

Note: The equivalence scale is calculated on the basis of 1 for a single person, 1.6 for a couple, plus 0.25 per child.

income, which is total net income divided by the number of equivalent adults in the family. The equivalence scale used is

1	for a single person
1.6	for a couple
0.25	for each child

This scale is only one of many that could reasonably be applied, and is intended only to illustrate the possibilities. One of the advantages of an interactive program is that the user can specify alternative equivalence scales. The scale means that a couple with net income of £80 find themselves in the range £43.25 to £55.15 a week, since their net equivalent income is £50 a week. The ranges in the tables have been chosen to give decile groups for net equivalent incomes before the policy change.

Turning to the results in Table 6.1, we see that the pattern of average gain or loss by decile groups is highly progressive. There is a gain of some £19 a week for the bottom decile. Put another way, the proportion of the population with net

Table 6.7 Partial basic income (Scheme B): distribution of gains and losses by decile group of before-reform equivalent income

Range of equivalent income, upper end (£)	Percentage in each row with changes (£ per week)						
	<−15	−5/−15	0/−5	No change	0/5	5/15	>15
43.25	0.08	1.69	1.36	1.05	10.09	34.41	51.32
55.15	0.28	4.35	9.70	5.37	22.02	25.01	33.27
65.80	0.24	0.90	6.71	8.14	37.63	22.69	23.39
78.05	0.14	1.40	10.66	5.01	22.68	30.42	29.69
93.00	0.00	3.17	9.56	0.18	13.57	40.69	32.83
109.85	0.14	9.48	10.44	0.22	42.07	21.80	15.85
130.80	2.85	22.83	31.45	1.18	21.91	16.57	3.21
159.90	24.00	46.82	17.25	0.17	5.38	5.11	1.27
204.70	64.96	31.20	2.17	0.01	0.64	0.96	0.06
—	94.95	4.63	0.27	0.00	0.00	0.00	0.15
Overall % in each range	18.74	12.64	9.97	2.13	17.60	19.80	19.12

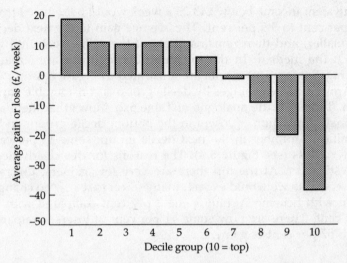

Fig. 6.3 Average gain from more redistributive BI/FT scheme by deciles

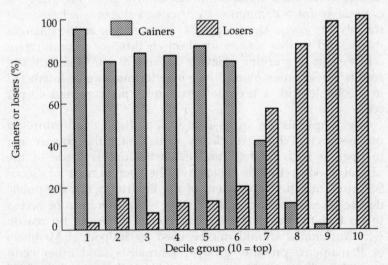

Fig. 6.4 Gainers/losers from more redistributive BI/FT scheme by deciles

equivalent income below £43.25 a week would be reduced from 10 per cent to 5.5 per cent. The average gain to the next decile is smaller, and then remains at about the same level until we reach the median. In the top three deciles there are sizeable average losses. The results are illustrated in Figure 6.3.

Around these averages by decile group is considerable variation. Table 6.7, the analogue of Table 6.2, shows that there are a small proportion of losers in the bottom decile group, and a significant number in the next decile group: some 15 per cent suffer a loss (see Figure 6.4). The reasons for this clearly need investigation. At the top there are very few gainers. Overall, there are, as we would expect, many fewer cases of 'no change' than with Scheme A: only some 2 per cent compared with 25 per cent. There are now some 41 per cent of losers, compared with 57 per cent of gainers.

6.7 Advantages and Disadvantages of Tax-Benefit Models

The speed with which these calculations can be done—the product of the new technology—has transformed the contribution which these models can make to the design of policy. It is possible for a committee to discuss a possible scheme, get the results, revise the proposals, have a look at the changes made, and in this way work through three or four different schemes in a morning. Having looked at the distributional results for Schemes A and B, we may for instance be interested in a scheme with a tax rate between 25 per cent and 40 per cent.

The emphasis on accessibility is a distinctive feature of our research. While it is clearly valuable for the government to operate such models (and extensive use is made of the official models by the Treasury, the Department of Social Security, and the Department of the Environment), the public debate takes on a further dimension when there can be access to tax-benefit models by outside bodies. There is no reason why our model should not be used by individual Members of Parliament, pressure groups, journalists, and other commentators. For example, it was possible at the time of the 1988 Budget—even with its extensive tax changes—to show the effect of the Chancellor's proposals within minutes of his sitting down.

TAXMOD does not merely produce numbers. It confronts the policy designer with questions that may not be apparent to her or him but which have to be answered before one can assess the implications. It is a valuable discipline in that proposals have to be fully specified. Indeed, every government should be required to convert its tax-benefit proposals into computer code before they are legislated! The process may also be valuable in suggesting policy options which were not previously apparent. For example, if child benefit were to be made taxable, this would still leave open in the case of a couple whether it is taxable as the income of the husband or the wife. TAXMOD forces the user to make a choice.

Of course, there are major limitations to the results. In particular, the model is based on a survey that is dated (the above results use data from 1982), which suffers from differential non-response (for example, because families with children are more likely to be at home when the FES interviewer calls than those without children), and where certain types of income are understated. Our research on TAXMOD, and now POLIMOD, has been particularly concerned with these problems. We make adjustments for underreported income using external evidence. We have devised a procedure for grossing up the survey data which brings them into line with a series of external control totals. This is very necessary. If for example one simply applies a uniform grossing-up factor, then the number of children is overstated by nearly a third, which would clearly lead to a large error in the estimate of the cost of child benefit.

These are problems which we have attempted to overcome; and our attempts to validate the results against other models and other estimates provides some ground for believing that we have been reasonably successful, although problems remain, notably in the treatment of the take-up of means-tested benefits. There are, however, certain things that the model does not attempt to do. Most importantly, the analysis is essentially arithmetic: i.e. we simply calculate the effect of the policy change without any attempt to predict the impact on behaviour. This is taken up again in Chapter 7.

7 Taxation and Work Incentives

7.1 Introduction

Empirical public finance has been a most active field of research in the past two decades, and a great deal has been learned from the application of econometric and experimental methods. In this chapter, I consider what can be deduced from this literature, and from the underlying theoretical framework, about the impact of income taxation on incentives. This is relevant because the flat tax associated with the basic income scheme is likely to be higher than the present marginal rates faced by many taxpayers, although the rise in tax rate is not, of course, the only change brought about by the Basic Income/Flat Tax (BI/FT) package. The replacement by the basic income of social insurance and social assistance benefits may also be expected to affect incentives (see, for example, Atkinson 1987, and Atkinson and Micklewright 1991). Reasons of space mean, however, that I have to limit the discussion to the effects of changes in income tax rates.

In focusing on work incentives, I am not suggesting that this is the only aspect of family behaviour potentially affected by the introduction of the BI/FT programme. The reform may, for instance, influence savings decisions, particularly the extent to which people make provision for old age. The existence of a basic income might be expected to reduce private provision but the replacement of social insurance benefits could have the reverse effect. At present people may believe that contributions to social insurance provide a guarantee of a retirement pension, whereas the level of a future basic income is less certain and more exposed to political risk. If the basic income promise is less credible than that made by social insurance, then people may save more in other forms. Moreover, to the extent that the BI/FT scheme reduces dependence on means-tested assistance in old age, it avoids the 'savings trap' which people face under such assistance. The latter means that there may be little or nothing to be gained from individual saving, on account of the way in which assets are taken into account when assessing assistance.

Another set of decisions which may be affected by the basic income are those regarding family and household formation. It is an important feature of the basic income that it is paid on an individual basis, in contrast to the family unit used in assessing social assistance entitlement. To the extent that the latter encouraged family dissolution, this disincentive may no longer be present. The basic income may also allow young people, at present often disqualified from benefit, to become independent of their parents.

These are important issues, but here I confine attention to what is probably the most discussed aspect of incentives—the effect on work decisions. Moreover, even here the treatment is selective. For example, I say little about the life-cycle aspects of labour supply, and the family dimension to decision-taking does not receive the attention which it deserves.

7.2 Different Dimensions of Labour Supply

The theoretical analysis of the BI/FT proposal in earlier chapters treated labour supply as a single variable, L, usually interpreted as hours of work. Individuals are assumed to be able to vary their hours freely in response to changes in the budget constraint that they face. In some cases, L falls to zero, in which case the person chooses not to participate in the paid labour force. It is these two aspects—hours of work and participation—that are the main focus of the review of empirical evidence in this chapter. It is, however, important to stress that there are many dimensions to labour supply, many more in fact than are typically taken into account in the empirical study of incentives.

First of all, it is not simply a question of the hours spent at work but also what the worker *does* during the work period. There is the dimension of effort, or how hard people work when they are actually there. In some cases, intensity of work is directly remunerated: for example where there is piece-work or payment by results. People are paid according to how much they produce, or on commission, or on a bonus scheme. In this situation, the actual hours may not be the key variable as much as the output; and the effect of taxation may be that people take it easier, producing less in the day—or the reverse. L may be taken as standing, not for hours, but for work effort.

Where there is no direct measurement, such as output, then work intensity may be harder to identify. For example, it has been alleged that managers in Britain are less willing to take responsibility, because the financial rewards are insufficient. The truth of such a claim is, of course, hard to investigate. In response to changes in taxation, people may be less willing to seek promotion, or to move from one job to another. Related are decisions about training and the choice of occupation. Suppose that people can choose between two jobs, one of which they can enter at once and the other of which involves a period of training. The second job must presumably offer a higher level of earnings to compensate for the training period. According to the simple theory of investment in human capital, for people to be indifferent it must be the case that the present discounted value of earnings must be the same in the two jobs. (There may also be differences in the non-pecuniary advantages which enter the calculation.) We have to ask how such choices are affected by proposals such as that for a BI/FT.

The example of training brings us back to the subject of participation. By going to college a person is postponing entry to the labour force and reducing the period of participation in the labour force. This may be placed in a life-cycle context, where the work career has to be seen as a whole. People may participate in the paid labour force for all their adult life; or they may spend periods caring for children or other dependants; or they may retire. There have in fact been major changes in the degree of participation in the labour force. In Britain, the participation rates for men have fallen substantially. In 1965, few men retired before the minimum retirement age for the state pension (65), and a sizeable minority of those above that age were in the labour force. A quarter of a century later, only a small percentage of men aged over 65 were in the labour force, and a third of those aged 55–64 were economically inactive. Participation has also been changing for women; indeed there has been an almost off-setting increase in their participation, although in Britain this takes in many cases the form of part-time work.

Finally, there is the question of emigration. This is a rather different dimension of labour supply response, but one which with the development of the common internal market in Europe seems likely to be increasingly important.

7.3 The Impact of Taxation on Labour Supply

The fact that there are many different dimensions of labour supply needs to be borne in mind when examining the potential impact of the BI/FT proposal. It is possible that the same considerations apply. In the case of the hours of work decision, there are the traditional income and substitution effects. The income effect stems from the fact that the tax makes people worse off, and if leisure is a normal good, this reduction in their real income causes them to consume less, so that to this extent the income tax acts as an incentive. The substitution effect stems from the fact that at the margin people are keeping less of every £1 earned, and this acts as a disincentive, causing them to move round the indifference curve in the direction of more leisure (the substitution effect being that which would arise if compensating adjustments were made for the income effect of the wage change, so that they stayed on the same indifference curve). The combined result is that taxation may cause people to work more hours, or fewer; it may cause them to refuse overtime or to seek it out; it may cause them to take unpaid leave or to work through their holidays for extra pay.

The ambiguity with respect to the effect of taxation amounts to the same as saying that the labour supply curve may slope upwards or backwards. In the simple iso-elastic labour supply function used as an example in Chapters 1–3, the income effect was assumed to be zero, so that the elasticity with respect to the net wage rate was necessarily positive, but in general both effects are in operation. In other words, in the iso-elastic case, with a proportional tax at rate t, we have

$$\log_e L = a + \varepsilon \log_e [w(1 - t)] - \beta \log_e M \qquad (7.1)$$

where M denotes income from non-labour sources, and the negative sign reflects the negative effect where leisure is a normal good. The parameter ε now measures the *total* wage elasticity of labour supply, and may now be positive or negative. (Whereas the *compensated* elasticity, moving round an indifference curve, must be positive.) In general, the total elasticity is equal to the substitution, or compensated, elasticity minus the marginal propensity to spend extra income on leisure. So that if the receipt of an extra £100 of unearned income causes a person to reduced his or her earnings by £20, and the compensated elasticity is 0.1, then the total elasticity is equal to $0.1 - 0.2 = -0.1$.

Politicians tend only to think of the substitution effect, but we have a theoretical ambiguity, where leisure is a normal good. Such an ambiguity is recognized in the responses made to interview studies of incentives: taxation is 'a two-edged sword. High deductions make you want to work more overtime to make up what you lose [*income effect*]—but if you get to a certain amount it's not worth working for [*substitution effect*]' (quoted by Brown and Levin 1974: 845, passages in square brackets added).

The same contraposition of income and substitution effects may apply to other dimensions of labour supply. The retirement decision is a case in point. The introduction of a BI/FT may lead to a person paying more tax, net of the basic income, whether continuing at work or retired on an occupational pension. The person may therefore feel less able to retire early (income effect). On the other hand, the proposal may reduce the financial attractiveness of additional earnings, and hence (substitution effect) make retirement more likely.

In other cases the effect may be different. For example, taxation may be a clear disincentive, as is illustrated by emigration. We would expect, other things equal, that a rise in income tax in Britain would make it more likely that people choose to work abroad. A tax increase, with no corresponding improvement in benefits from government spending, would therefore reduce the labour supplied in Britain. This is not to say that taxation is a powerful influence. In the case of the brain drain, scientists often say that it is not the net salary that is decisive but the provision of laboratories, equipment, etc.

But in so far as net salaries are relevant, then the impact of taxation is negative. Conversely, improvements in social security benefits may have the reverse effect, making Britain more attractive, other things equal.

A second example where the effect may be different from that predicted by the standard analysis is that of the effect on human capital decisions, where it has been argued that the income tax discriminates against such investment. According to Schultz, the US tax system is such that 'our tax laws everywhere discriminate against human capital' (1961: 13). But one has to be careful in making such an assertion, as was pointed out by Boskin (1975*b*) and Rosen (1980). If the decision is based solely on comparing the expected gain in earnings with the earnings foregone while training, a tax which is simply proportional would reduce both by the same percentage, and the balance in the equation is unaffected. If the tax is at rate t, we would simply have a factor $(1 - t)$ appearing on both sides. It is only to the extent that the tax has a graduated marginal rate, falling more heavily on the earnings of trained labour, that the return to training is reduced. Of course this is an over-simplified representation, and costs such as university fees may well not be tax-deductible, but the essential point is that human capital investment largely takes the form of foregone earnings, so that if these earnings would have been taxed, the *cost* of the investment is reduced as well as the benefits.

This is relevant to the choice between the BI/FT scheme and the present graduated structure, where a flat rate of 40 per cent may be less of a discouragement to human capital investment than a rate of 20 per cent followed by one of 40 per cent. For those who can 'borrow' (by foregoing earnings) in a tax-deductible way, a higher rate of tax on these foregone earnings reduces the net cost. It may also be the case that the basic income, by cashing out the tax allowances, helps people finance their period of full-time education. Students would not simply pay no income tax; they would receive the basic income. Where there are limits to the amount that students can borrow, this may be a very real advantage.

Yet another decision which may be affected differently is that concerning work effort. Suppose that, as in the efficiency wage theory discussed in Chapter 5, there are primary sector jobs in which people can 'shirk' if their work performance is not monitored. Monitoring is not certain, so that people face some probability of being caught shirking. If they are caught, then they are fired and have to make do with lower wage employment in the secondary sector. Employers have to pay a higher wage w_y, using the same notation as in Chapter 5, to make sure that people do not shirk and put in the necessary effort, at a cost which we call e. There is an exogenous probability q of being monitored. The primary sector worker is assumed to weigh the certainty of $(w_y - e)$ if he puts in effort against the probability $(1 - q)$ of w_y plus the probability q of being fired and earning $(w_x - e)$ in the secondary sector. (It is assumed for convenience that workers are risk neutral and consider only income in a single period.) The wage premium necessary to just induce effort is

$$w_y = w_x + (e/q)(1 - q) \tag{7.2}$$

A proportional tax on income reduces both net wages but has no effect on effort. The impact of the tax must therefore be to widen the wage differential between the primary and secondary sectors, increasing it to $1/(1 - t)$ times its previous value. In this respect, we are tracing through the implications of the workers' change in behaviour for the labour market as a whole.

The reference to primary sector employment brings me to the point that a number of dimensions of labour supply may not be the subject of individual decision; rather they are covered by collective agreements negotiated between unions and management. The number of hours worked by office staff in universities is laid down by a collective agreement, as is the number of days of holiday. An individual cannot unilaterally decide to work a sixty-hour week, nor typically to take thirteen weeks' vacation. This does not mean that taxes and benefits have no effect, but it does mean that the decisions to be studied are not just individual ones but also those reached via collective negotiations. In the latter case, if taxes cause individual members to want to work shorter hours, then this may lead them to put pressure on their union executive, but it will depend on a majority being affected in the same way. If people do not like the decision made by the union, they may be able to take another job, but the scope for this is limited.

Finally, we have to recognize that people may not in fact be on their supply curves, in the sense that they would like to work more hours at the going wage. In the dual labour market, as examined in Chapter 5, there may be an equilibrium situation where workers would prefer to work in the primary sector but have to queue among the unemployed. This in effect means that their choices are rationed. A trade union may negotiate a combination of wage rate and hours such that their members would prefer to work more hours at that wage. This can come about where the union is concerned about the total level of employment (Oswald and Walker 1993). In such situations, we may draw misleading conclusions if we treat the observed hours purely as the result of utility maximizing choice faced with a linear budget constraint. It is the theory as well as the evidence that is open to question.

7.4 Sources of Empirical Evidence

Empirical evidence about labour supply comes from a variety of different types of source:

- questionnaire studies involving individual self-testimony
- experiments involving individuals
- cross-country comparisons of aggregate behaviour
- time-series of aggregate behaviour
- cross-section data on individuals based on sample surveys or administrative records.

To an outside observer, the simplest approach to the empirical investigation of labour supply may be to ask the subjects themselves. Just as market research asks people about their choice of newspaper or holiday destination, so too we could ask them about how they make their work decisions and what role is played by taxation and benefits. What were the factors uppermost in their mind when they decided to change career? Why did they decide to take early retirement? Just as market research asks people about potential new products, to see if there is a market, so too we could ask how people think they would react to changes in taxation or transfers, such as the introduction of a BI/FT scheme.

For the responses to this kind of questionnaire study to be informative, several conditions would have to be satisfied. First, the respondents would have to understand the question. We are dealing with a complex area. It would not be easy to communicate the essentials of the BI/FT scheme in a way that people could grasp. Secondly, people have to be able to assess their own motives and articulate their response. Reactions to taxation may be instinctive, rather than calculated. Decisions like that of changing one's job may be the result of a number of factors, the relative importance of which it may not be easy for the respondent to determine. Thirdly, even if they know the answer, respondents may not always convey the truth. A person may attribute early retirement to penal higher rates of taxation, because he regards this as a socially acceptable reason, whereas in fact the main motivation is that he has taken up golf.

A good example of the use of self-testimony is provided by the work of Brown and Levin (1974), who in 1971 studied the decision whether to work overtime by weekly-paid workers in the United Kingdom. After a large number of questions which did not mention taxation, they asked whether it had led them to work more, less, or 'doesn't apply/neither'. Omitting those whose answers were felt to be implausible, Brown and Levin found that as many as 69 per cent reported no effect. On the basis of the average hours of overtime worked by different respondents, they conclude that the aggregate impact of income taxation on overtime working is small. A similar conclusion was reached in the United States. As summarized by Pechman, 'Nearly all people who are asked about income taxation grumble about it, but relatively few state that they work fewer hours or exert less than their best efforts to avoid tax' (1971: 66). It is not, however, possible to determine whether this is due to the cancellation of income and substitution effects or to their small absolute magnitude.

Experimental Evidence

The remaining sources of evidence about taxation and benefits treat people essentially as dumb animals from whom we can learn by observing their actual behaviour, but no notice is taken of any explanation that the subjects offer for their behaviour. The parallel with animal science suggests that the obvious way in which to generate such evidence is by means of a controlled experiment. There has indeed been considerable recent interest in experimental economics. Most of this research has involved 'artificial' experiments, in the sense that the decision-making takes place within the laboratory, and is not part of everyday life. Rather different are experiments which present people with a changed tax and benefit schedule and observe how real-world decisions are affected.

It is possible for example to imagine an experiment in which a representative sample of families are faced with a BI/FT schedule of taxes and benefits and their behaviour over, say, a three-year period is compared with that of a control sample. Such experiments have been undertaken in the United States and Canada regarding the negative income tax, and these are one of the major sources of evidence regarding labour supply elasticities. In the New Jersey experiment in 1968–72, for example, eight negative income tax plans were studied, with guaranteed incomes ranging from 50 to 125 per cent of the poverty line, and marginal tax rates at which the benefit was withdrawn varying between 30 and 70 per cent.

Experimental evidence has to be interpreted with care. There are several reasons why an experiment of this kind cannot capture the full effect of the reform if actually introduced. The experiment is of limited duration; and people may react in a manner different from how they would if they expected it to be permanent. The experiment applies only to a sample of people, so that collective responses may not show up. None the less, the negative income tax experiments have added greatly to our understanding of labour supply, and some of the main findings are summarized in the next section.

'Natural Experiments'

The limited scope for carrying out experiments like those with the negative income tax means that we have to rely mainly on 'natural experiments' generated for us in the real world, such as those when different governments set different tax rates. Such natural experiments have the advantage that they typically affect the population as a whole; they may also be expected to be longer-lasting than those conducted by researchers. There is, however, the basic question as to how far they are indeed 'experiments'.

The most obvious example is provided by the comparison of different countries. We observe that Sweden, say, has typically set higher income tax rates than the United States. Can we examine the labour supply in Sweden, compared to the United States, and draw conclusions about the impact of taxation? If Swedish doctors play more tennis and see fewer patients (a purely hypothetical statement), is this evidence that progressive taxation reduces work effort? The problem with such an inference is that we have no idea what other factors may be influencing labour supply decisions. There may, similarly, be common influences on both variables. There may be economic, social, or cultural factors which lead to differences in labour supply and which also lead to differences in the tax and other policy choices, without there necessarily being any direct causal connection between taxation and labour supply. We do not have a *controlled* experiment.

The same objection applies to the time-series studies. We may observe that tax rates have fallen over the past twenty years, and that hours of work have also decreased. It does not follow that we can conclude that taxation was an incentive to work. Again, other variables are changing. Set in a supply and demand framework, the effect of tax cuts may have been to raise real disposable wage rates, and to induce people to offer more labour at a given pre-tax wage, but the demand curve may also have shifted. The fall in hours may reflect the recession rather than tax cuts. (This raises again the question as to whether people are working as much as they would choose.)

Cross-section Evidence

The time-series and cross-country evidence is also typically limited in that it relates to *aggregate* evidence, such as average hours of work of all workers. Yet there may be heterogeneous responses. We have seen that the participation rates of men and women have moved differently over time; and they may not respond in the same way to changes in taxation or transfers. Union and non-union workers may respond differently (Oswald and Walker 1993). Tax policy does not affect all groups uniformly, and it is the nature of the BI/FT proposal that it will have differential impacts on net incomes and marginal tax rates (as illustrated numerically in the previous chapter). For this reason, much of the research of the past two decades has used cross-section data, that is data from surveys or administrative records on individuals or families, which allow us to explore the relation with individual tax and benefit position.

Ideally, cross-section data on individuals permit us to control for the individual characteristics and circumstances which affect their labour supply decisions. The problem is that the analysis may be controlled, but it is not an *experiment*, in that there is not typically exogenous variation in the tax or benefit parameters. If all respondents are living in the same jurisdiction, then differences in individual tax rate or benefit receipt are attributable to differences in individual characteristics which may need to be included as explanatory variables in the model in their own right. Where there is joint taxation of married couples, a woman may face a higher marginal rate of tax because her husband has high earnings, but the level of the husband's earnings may also influence her decision as to how many hours to work. In this case, the mediating variable is observable, and it may be possible to model this interaction, but where it is not observable then we may be confounding the effect of differences in policy variables with that of the unobserved personal characteristics.

It is important therefore to ask the question, what is the experiment being performed? The answer does not necessarily mean that we cannot proceed. Exogenous variation may, for instance, be present if there is geographical variation in tax and benefit parameters (providing that geographical variables do not also enter the explanation of behaviour), as with unemployment insurance in the USA. It may be present where the sample is drawn from a number of years spanning a policy change in tax or benefit programmes. We then have a mixture of cross-section and time-series evidence. There may also be exogenous random variation caused by administrative error and discretion.

Conclusion

These different sources of evidence are sometimes seen in adversarial terms, with one group of authors making use of one type of evidence and a rival group espousing another. In my' view, however, they should rather be seen as complementary. The variety of dimensions of labour supply is a good example why different sources may give us different results about the effects of taxation without there being any conflict or paradox involved.

7.5 Evidence about Taxation and Labour Supply

Empirical analysis of labour supply has been an intensive area of research in the past two decades, particularly in the United States to which the evidence cited here pertains (unless otherwise stated). (Evidence for European countries is surveyed in Atkinson and Mogensen 1993.) There has been considerable progress in the methods applied, progress which is reflected in the use of the terms 'first generation' and 'second generation' to distinguish studies made before the early 1970s from the subsequent ones (Killingsworth 1983), with the influential collection of papers edited by Cain and Watts (1973) marking the watershed. Over the same period, views have changed about the effect of taxation. The prevailing judgement before the 1980s was that labour supply had little impact on work decisions; a decade later it was widely held that taxation represented a serious disincentive. This shift no doubt reflected changing political attitudes, but a role was also played by academic research, parts of which was widely quoted in public debate, notably Hausman (1981).

The new research is based both on new techniques and new data, which are discussed in turn. In order to provide a focus for this discussion, I take a labour supply model such as that set out earlier, with the addition of a stochastic term, u:

$$\log_e L_i = a + \varepsilon \log_e [w(1 - t)]_i - \beta \log_e M_i + u_i$$
$$\equiv \log_e L_i^* + u_i \qquad (7.3)$$

where a subscript i has been incorporated, to denote the labour supply, net wage, and income, of person i. The interpretation of the stochastic term is often not discussed. It may represent measurement error, in that L_i^* is the actual labour supply, but there is a multiplicative error in recording hours in our data source, where this error varies randomly across individuals. It may reflect the failure of the person to find a job offering the desired hours of work, or optimization error. A second, quite different interpretation, however, is that the stochastic term is an *individual fixed effect*. On this basis, u_i being large means that person i has an unusually strong preference for work, given his or her net wage rate and income. This distinction between the interpretations of u_i plays a role in what follows.

New Estimation Techniques

The aim of the second-generation studies has been to resolve some of the major analytical and statistical issues which arise in seeking to estimate labour supply responses. There have been a number of excellent surveys of this literature (see, for example, Brown 1983, Killingsworth 1983, Pencavel 1986, Pudney 1989, ch. 5, and Blundell 1988 and 1992). It is not my purpose here to review the full range of issues, rather to give a flavour of some of the most significant: the treatment of non-linear budget constraints, sample selection, and the endogeneity of explanatory variables.

The typical graduated income tax schedule involves a series of brackets where the marginal rate of tax is higher in successive brackets. This generates a budget constraint like *OABCD* drawn in Figure 7.1 (similar to Figure 3.1). As a consequence, the marginal return to working depends on the number of hours worked. It is possible to see the hours L_i and net income N_i chosen by person i in Figure 7.1 as the choice made by that person if faced with the linear budget constraint *YZ* (marked with a dashed line): i.e. with a marginal tax rate, t_2, corresponding to that bracket, and with a 'virtual' lump-sum income

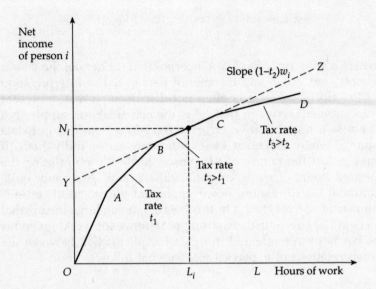

Fig. 7.1 Non-linear budget constraint

Y, calculated as $N_i - (1 - t_2)w_iL_i$. The difficulty is that this virtual income, and the marginal tax rate, depend on the choice made by the individual. They cannot be treated as parametric to the problem. A person with a taste for hard work will be observed to have high earnings and to have a high marginal tax rate. We cannot draw any direct inferences from a comparison with a person who enjoys fishing and is found on the segment with a low marginal tax rate. Put another way, we cannot treat the marginal tax rate as varying exogenously in the population, like a kind of experiment; it depends on u_i.

The typical income tax schedule generates a non-linear but *convex* budget constraint. The payment of income-tested benefits, on the other hand, may lead to non-convexities. The withdrawal of benefits as earnings rise mean that marginal tax rates may be higher at low earnings than further up the scale. There is then the possibility of discontinuities in the labour supply function, in that we would not expect to observe people choosing certain points on the budget constraint.

One of the areas of micro-econometric research has been to

develop techniques for dealing with such non-linearities: see Burtless and Hausman (1978), Hausman (1981 and 1985), Brown (1980, ch. 5), and Wales and Woodland (1979). These involve an explicit treatment of utility maximization over a non-linear budget set, and, in the case of non-convexities, the comparison of different discrete points. (The parameters are estimated by maximizing the likelihood function formed by making assumptions about the distribution of u_i.) Such a treatment typically takes as a maintained hypothesis that the individual is fully informed about the after-tax budget constraint. In applying this approach, the interpretation of u_i is relevant, since if it is a taste difference between people, then it may be expected to affect the probability that they are located at different points (which may allow the variance of this element to be estimated).

A reference point in this field is provided by the widely cited results of Hausman (1981). He estimated a linear labour supply function (i.e. replacing $\log_e L_i$ by L_i on the left-hand side of (7.3), and similarly for the net wage and income variables) using data for 1975 from the University of Michigan Panel Study on Income Dynamics. In considering his results, it is important to bear in mind that he allows preferences in the form of the income response to vary across the population, and finds substantial variation around a median of approximately 0.55, with the value of the parameter constrained to be non-negative. (This value is calculated using the information contained in n. 42 of Hausman (1981) and the mean net wage calculated by Pencavel (1986, n. 78).) Pencavel (1986: 65) draws attention to the high estimated propensity to spend additional unearned income on leisure: the median implying that the effect of an extra $100 is that the person reduces his or her earnings by $55, and the quartile range is from $23 to $109, the latter implying that total net income falls. It may be debated whether it is appropriate to constrain this parameter to be non-negative in all cases.

The income response is important, since in the case of married men the measured total elasticity is close to zero. This means that the compensated elasticity is of a similar absolute magnitude to the income response, and hence for many people is estimated to be substantial. As Hausman comments, 'taxation has important effects on labor supply' (1981: 53). For wives, he finds a total elasticity of between 0.9 and 1.0; and the estimated wage elasticities for female household heads are midway between those of husbands and those of wives. It should be noted that these estimates have been questioned by several writers (see Heckman 1983 and 1993, and MaCurdy *et al.* 1990), who have argued that the findings are sensitive to the specification of the model. A simple functional form, like that used illustratively here, has obvious advantages but may well impose too tight a strait-jacket on empirical data, leading to fragile parameter estimates. Alternative specifications of the labour supply of married women in the UK are examined by Blundell *et al.* (1988); a non-parametric approach, not based on a tightly specified functional form, is described by Duncan and Jones (1994).

The findings of Hausman contributed to alarmist views being expressed about the impact of taxation on work incentives; the estimated elasticities for men are, however, distinctly higher than those in a number of other studies. The summary given by Burtless (1986, Table 3) of twenty-six estimates of male labour supply surveyed by Killingsworth (1983) shows an average total elasticity of around −0.10, and a compensated elasticity of 0.28. There was, however, considerable variation, the standard deviation of the latter being 0.42. The range of results obtained in different studies for both men and women is indeed bewildering to the outside observer, who would like to know how far these differences are due to differences in the data, in the choice of functional form, in the treatment of the budget constraint, in the specification of the stochastic term, or in the method of estimation. It is rare for findings to be reported in a form which facilitates comparison across studies. I have sympathy with the *cri du cœur* of Pencavel in his survey article:

It is impossible for me to graph each fitted hours of work equation as a function of the observed value taken by the variables of interest. Yet this is exactly what is needed for a full understanding of the implications of any given set of estimates. Unfortunately, only rarely are such graphs presented. The normal substitute is to present the implied values of the behavior responses calculated at sample mean values or, less frequently, the average of the behavioral responses calculated for each observation. Some papers do not even do this. (1986: 55)

As he notes, elasticities calculated (as here) at sample means or medians may be quite unrepresentative of the whole distribution (on this point see, in another context, Atkinson *et al.* 1990).

Labour Supply of Married Women

In this respect, the investigation by Mroz (1987) is of particular value. He examines the labour supply responses of married women using a single data set, and a common functional form (linear in hours and income, log-linear in the net wage) but systematically comparing a range of different approaches. He uses, like Hausman (1981), data for 1975 from the University of Michigan Panel Study on Income Dynamics. The focus on married women is of interest in view of the widespread belief that their labour supply is more sensitive to taxation. According to Killingsworth's survey in 1983, 'most of the available evidence suggests that female labour supply, measured either as labour force participation or as hours of work, is considerably more wage and property income elastic than male labour supply' (1983: 432). The forty-eight studies of women surveyed by him (summarized by Burtless (1986, Table 3) showed an average total elasticity of 2.0, with the compensated elasticity being essentially the same (the income response being zero).

Mroz considers, in addition to the role of taxes, the problems of the endogeneity of the gross wage and controlling for self-selection into the labour force. These problems may be briefly illustrated by examples. Commonly average hourly wages are not directly observed, but calculated by dividing total earnings by reported hours. Any error in the measurement of hours induces a spurious negative correlation between hours and the measured wage rate. Sample selection bias is illustrated by the example of married women where a sizeable proportion may not be working (an issue raised by Gronau (1973) and Heckman (1974)). If no information is available about the wage rates of those women with zero hours, they cannot be included in an equation like (7.3). However, this is equivalent to omitting those observations where the value of u_i is less than $-\log_e L_i^*$. So if u_i in the population as a whole has zero mean this will not be true for the sample used in estimation. The latter includes disproportionately people with a positive optimization error or strong taste for work.

All of these problems are matters which have to be tested in econometric research. The empirical analysis of Mroz reveals that the effects are of some subtlety. Two studies may give similar results on account of the cancellation of two opposing effects, which may not be true in other contexts. On the basis of his systematic consideration of different cases, he finds that for the range of specifications that cannot be rejected there is a narrow range of estimates of income and substitution effects. Moreover these 'are small and precise' (1987: 791). Of the twenty-seven estimates which pass the specification tests, the largest point estimate corresponds to a total elasticity (at the sample mean annual hours) of some 0.12; the maximum upper bound of the 95 per cent confidence intervals is around 0.45. He concludes that, as far as *working* married women are concerned, the earlier findings of large elasticities are misleading: 'we are able to obtain large estimates of the income and wage coefficients. Our statistical tests, however, emphatically reject the economic and statistical assumptions needed to obtain these large wage and income effects' (1987: 795). This evidence for the United States suggests that the total elasticity with respect to wages of the hours of work of working women is closer to 0 than to 1; and the same has been reported for the United Kingdom (Blundell 1992: 27).

Negative Income Tax (NIT) Experiments in the United States

Much the same conclusion regarding the importance of participation decisions has been reached using the new data source which became available as a result of the NIT experiments. In broad terms, as summarized by Burtless and Haveman,

The results from the largest and most sophisticated of the NIT experiments showed that youths and women, in particular, cut back their activity in the labour market, especially if they were enrolled in the longer-term, five-year plans. Prime-aged men reduced their annual hours of work by 9 or 10 per cent; their spouses reduced annual hours by 17 to 20 per cent; and single women heading families reduced

Table 7.1 Summary of estimated labour supply responses in NIT experiments in the United States

	Elasticity of annual hours with respect to net wage rate	
	Total elasticity	Compensated elasticity
Men (weighted average of 21 estimates)	−0.02	0.09
Wives (weighted average of 14 estimates excluding New Jersey)	0.17	0.24
Female family heads (weighted average of 11 estimates)	−0.04	0.14

Source: Burtless 1986, Table 3.

annual hours by more than 20 per cent—by as much as 28 to 32 per cent in the longer-duration plans. Much of the work reduction occurred in the form of withdrawals from employment or active labor force participation rather than in marginal reductions in weekly work effort. (1987a: 47)

In the case of a negative income tax, the income and substitution effects operate in the same direction, both tending to reduce labour supply. In order to separate these effects, the NIT data have been further analysed by estimating labour supply models, such as that set out earlier. The summary by Burtless (1986) of the findings of different studies based on the NIT data over the period 1968 to 1982 is shown in Table 7.1. It may be seen that the estimated compensated elasticities are largest for wives, but in all cases small. Burtless draws attention to the difference between these findings and the labour supply elasticities assumed by Browning and Johnson in their work (1984) to which reference was made in Chapter 1. The functional form employed by these authors gives an overall total elasticity of 0.204 and a compensated elasticity of 0.312 (1984, Table 4), but for the bottom quintile these rise to 0.435 and 0.513. These are noticeably higher than the estimates shown in Table 7.1 and does not accord with the description of their elasticities as 'moderate' by Meltzer (1991: 16 n.).

The NIT experiments are generally considered to have reduced the range of uncertainty surrounding the response of hours of work to taxation, although the qualifications listed in the previous section must be borne in mind. Moreover, there is no necessary reason to expect the results to apply equally in a European context. Those interested in a BI/FT scheme in Europe might like to consider launching such an experimental research project, which would serve both to throw light on the economic effects of the reform and to demonstrate how it would work in reality.

7.6 Labour Supply and Tax-Benefit Models

The tax model, TAXMOD, used in Chapter 6 takes no account of changes in behaviour. This is a significant omission, since one of the avowed aims of tax reform is to change taxpayer behaviour, and it is patently not sufficient to assume that pretax incomes would be the same under the BI/FT structure as under the present system. The incorporation of behavioural changes into simulation models has been an important part of the research agenda in the UK of the Institute for Fiscal Studies (see for example Blundell *et al.* 1988) and other researchers (Pudney and Sutherland 1994). In the United States, progress in this direction has been rather slow: 'in comparison to the large number of studies of experimental labor supply response, there have been only few studies attempting to generalize the findings from the experiments to the U.S. population' (Burtless 1986: 38). One of the reasons has already been noted in Chapter 1: the empirical evidence is often limited to subgroups of the population.

Changes in behaviour affect both the revenue calculations and the evaluation of the welfare consequences for individual taxpayers. The impact on revenue follows from the labour supply function, which we take for purposes of exposition to be of the iso-elastic form (7.3). This may be used to predict for an individual taxpayer the change in earned income arising from a variation in the tax structure and hence the impact on total revenue. In order to evaluate the welfare consequences for an individual taxpayer, we need the indirect utility function (see Chapter 2):

$$V = \frac{L_0}{(1 + \varepsilon)}[w(1 - t)]^{1+\varepsilon} + M \tag{7.4}$$

where t is the tax rate on the relevant segment of the budget constraint and M is virtual income. In this special case, the level of welfare is equal to

$$V = \frac{1}{(1 + \varepsilon)}w(1 - t)L + M \tag{7.5}$$

so that labour income is in effect 'discounted' by a factor $1/(1 + \varepsilon)$ to allow for the cost of effort. It may be noted that I have taken here the least concave representation of the indirect utility function, and that the marginal utility of income is equal to unity at all levels of w and M.

The incorporation of behavioural responses into tax models poses a number of problems; here I would like to concentrate on the problem of communicating the results to a wider public. Equations are commonplace in academic journals, but they arouse suspicion in many quarters outside academic life. However, the complexities embedded in equations are not easily avoided. For example the idea of a proportional adjustment to earned income for the cost of effort in equation (7.5) is a quite intuitive one, and could easily be explained in words, but this is a consequence of the particular choice of functional form, and for more general formulations such an interpretation is not likely to be available.

Nor is this the only difference likely to arise. There is for instance the issue of the interpretation of the stochastic term in equation (7.3), which becomes particularly important once we leave the context of a simple linear model, as we obviously have to in the present application. If the departure of the observed labour supply from that predicted is an individual fixed effect, then it enters the determination of the person's response to changes in taxation. On the other hand, if the stochastic term reflects random optimization error or transitory variations, then there is a distribution of u_i for each individual. If we are concerned to calculate expected gross income, or expected revenue, then we have to allow for this distribution. In terms of expected indirect utility, the impact of the tax reform is diffused throughout the population. More generally, the stochastic term may be a combination of individual fixed effect and transitory variation.

The difference in conclusions means in turn that it is essential to communicate to users the interpretation which has been given to the stochastic term and its implications for the results. This is not easily done. It is noteworthy that Hausman, who has provided an extensive discussion of the treatment of the stochastic term in simulation (1983), when it comes to analysing the US tax reform for a more popular audience (Hausman and Poterba 1987), takes an 'average married man' and an 'average married woman', which side-steps the problem. Similarly, in the UK, Blundell *et al.* provide a clear account of their procedure (which assumes that the error term is a fixed effect) in their article in the *Journal of Public Economics* (1988), but the assumption is not typically referred to in more policy-oriented writing based on the analysis.

This is but one of several examples which could be given as to why the incorporation of behavioural responses into empirical tax models is a more complex matter than it may at first appear. I feel therefore that there is need for caution. This should not be taken as saying that behavioural responses are unimportant. Indeed, it can be claimed that public economics discovered the supply side of the economy before it became fashionable.

7.7 Concluding Comments

The relationship between taxation, benefits, and work incentives is a complex one. There are many dimensions to work decisions and these may be affected in different ways. It is not possible to make simple statements as to what may be predicted on theoretical grounds. Not even the direction of the effect of taxation on labour supply can be determined, since there are conflicting influences on most individual decisions. Empirical evidence cannot settle the issue definitively: 'there are *no* studies of labour supply that are not open to serious objection on at least one important ground' (Brown 1983: 167). Moreover, much of the research refers to the 1970s, and taxpayer responses may have changed over twenty years. The finding that hours of work of those at work are relatively unaffected by taxation, for example, may apply less to a labour force where union coverage is declining and where labour contracts are becoming more flexible.

While this does not mean that we can learn nothing from empirical studies, we certainly have to be cautious about the idea that their findings can be incorporated routinely into the analysis of policy. Policy-makers may be taking a serious gamble if they base plans for tax and benefit reform on predictions of increased labour supply (and tax revenue). This applies particularly to a proposal like the BI/FT scheme, which could take us far from the present position.

8 Concluding Reflection: The Integration of Public Economics

As explained in Chapter 1, it has not been my purpose in this book to argue for or against the Basic Income/Flat Tax proposal. In my view, it should definitely be on the agenda for public discussion, and there are certainly circumstances in which it would be, in my judgement, the best way to develop the tax and social security system in the European Union. My concern here, however, has been with the contribution that public economics can make to identifying these circumstances, and with the role which it can play in clarifying public debate on this important topic.

This in turn leads me to draw certain conclusions about the present state of the academic subject of public economics. In the course of the individual chapters, I have tried to highlight some of the areas where further research is much needed. These include the design of tax policy with non-welfarist objectives, the formalization of public choice theories, building general equilibrium models of incidence that take account of recent developments in the theory of labour markets, the incorporation of behavioural response into simulation models, and the study of aspects of household behaviour other than hours of work and participation.

At the same time, there is one overarching theme that I would like to stress: the need for greater integration of the different branches of the subject. This is set out schematically in Figure 8.1, which shows the subject divided into four main areas: design of policy (Chapters 2 and 3), public choice (Chapter 4), theory of incidence (Chapter 5), and empirical analysis (Chapters 6 and 7). Of the six possible pairings, at least four warrant, in my view, closer integration.

The first of these links is that between the design of policy

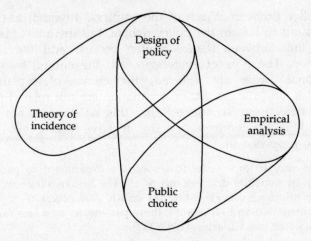

Fig. 8.1 Need for closer integration of different branches of public economics

and public choice theory. Convincing reasons have been put forward by public choice theorists for the study of the process of government decision-making, and the design of policy, or the policy framework, needs to take this into account. This aspect has already been described. Equally, from Chapter 5, it should be clear that the incidence, and hence the design, of policy can be very different once we leave the standard Arrow– Debreu model of the economy. In a world with segmented labour markets, efficiency wages, and involuntary unemployment, policy variables can have an impact unlike that typically assumed in the optimum taxation literature. The consequences of minimum wage legislation, not considered here, are a case in point. A start has been made in examining the design of policy in such richer models of the labour market, and in models of imperfect competition, but this field needs more systematic study.

The third link has not been identified earlier as such, which is that between the design of policy and the assembly of empirical evidence. In the literature on labour supply reviewed in Chapter 7, there has been a curious divorce between the estimation of parameters relevant to policy and the posing of the policy problem. Much of the empirical research has been carried out to inform the policy debate, but there has been no direct link between the estimation process and the design of policy. The type of evidence used, the criteria by which functional forms are selected, the choice of explanatory variables, and the estimation technique, are not related to the policy objectives. To suggest that this be done is not new. Stafford, in his comments on the negative income tax experiments, proposed that

Another way to proceed is to regard the experiment as part of a problem in statistical decision theory. . . . The first two ingredients in such an approach are: (1) listing the critical parameters about which we are uncertain and (2) relating these parameters to a loss function for policy-decision variables. (1985: 113)

It may well be for example that the losses from underestimating the elasticity of labour supply are greater than those from overestimating its value: i.e. that the loss function is not symmetric. Zellner and Rossi (1986) have spelled out further the requisites for such a decision-theoretic approach adopting a Bayesian method. Whatever method be followed, there is a strong case for a unified approach to the estimation and policy design processes. Estimation should not be carried out in isolation.

Finally, we have the link between empirical evidence and public choice. There can be little doubt that certain empirical studies, such as that by Hausman (1981) in the United States, have received wide attention in the public debate. The use of scientific research in the policy process is an interesting field to explore with regard to taxation and social policy; and it may be that the empirical research in turn needs to be conducted with an explicit concern for the public impact.

In sum, public economics has grown a great deal in the past twenty-five years, but has also become more fragmented. Such specialization reflects the deepening of our knowledge, and the fact that public policy issues rightly attract the attention of those whose field of specialism is outside public economics (such as micro-econometrics or labour economics). But it has costs, and there is a definite need today for closer integration of the different aspects which I have covered in this book.

References

Aaron, H. A. (1989), 'Politics and the professors revisited', *American Economic Review*, 79 (Papers and proceedings), 1–15.

Alesina, A. (1988), 'Credibility and policy convergence in a two-party system with rational voters', *American Economic Review*, 78: 796–805.

Agell, J., and Lundborg, P. (1992), 'Fair wages, involuntary unemployment and tax policies in the simple general equilibrium model', *Journal of Public Economics*, 47: 299–320.

Akerlof, G. A. (1978), 'The economics of "tagging" as applied to the optimal income tax, welfare programs, and manpower planning', *American Economic Review*, 68: 8–19.

Atkinson, A. B. (1969), *Poverty in Britain and the Reform of Social Security*, Cambridge University Press, Cambridge.

—— (1972), 'Maxi min and optimal income taxation', paper presented at Budapest Meeting of the Econometric Society, published in French in *Cahiers du Séminaire d'Économétrie*, 16 (1975).

—— (1973), 'How progressive should income tax be?', in M. Parkin and A. R. Nobay (eds.), *Essays in Modern Economics*, Longmans, London.

—— (1987), 'Income maintenance and social insurance: a survey', in A. Auerbach and M. S. Feldstein (eds.), *Handbook of Public Economics*, ii, North-Holland, Amsterdam.

—— (1988), 'The economics of unemployment insurance', Presidential Address to Econometric Society.

—— (1989), 'The costs of social dividend and tax credit schemes', in A. B. Atkinson, *Poverty and Social Security*, Harvester Press, Hemel Hempstead.

—— (1990), 'Public economics and the economic public', *European Economic Review*, 34: 225–48.

—— (1991a), 'Basic income schemes and the lessons from public economics', in K. J. Arrow (ed.), *Issues in Contemporary Economics*, i: *Markets and Welfare*, Macmillan, London.

—— (1991b), 'Social insurance', *Geneva Papers on Risk and Insurance Theory*, 16: 113–31.

—— (1992), 'Institutional features of unemployment insurance and the working of the labour market', in P. Dasgupta, D. Gale, O. Hart, and E. Maskin (eds.), *Economic Analysis of Markets and Games*, MIT Press, Cambridge, Mass.

—— Gomulka, J., and Stern, N. H. (1990), 'Spending on alcohol', *Economic Journal*, 100: 808–27.

—— and Micklewright, J. (1991), 'Unemployment compensation and labor market transitions: a critical review', *Journal of Economic Literature*, 29: 1679–727.

—— —— (1992), *Economic Transformation in Eastern Europe and the Distribution of Income*, Cambridge University Press, Cambridge.

—— and Mogensen, G. V. (1993) (eds.), *Welfare and Work Incentives*, Oxford University Press, Oxford.

—— and Stiglitz, J. E. (1980), *Lectures on Public Economics*, McGraw-Hill, New York.

—— and Sutherland, H. (1988), *Tax-Benefit Models*, ST/ICERD Occasional Paper 10, LSE.

—— —— (1989), 'Analysis of a partial basic income scheme', in A. B. Atkinson, *Poverty and Social Security*, Harvester Press, Hemel Hempstead.

—— —— (1990), 'Scaling the "poverty mountain": methods to extend incentives to all workers', in A. Bowen and K. Mayhew (eds.), *Improving Incentives for the Low-Paid*, Macmillan, London.

Aumann, R. J., and Kurz, M. (1977), 'Power and taxes', *Econometrica*, 45: 1137–61.

Barry, B. (1965), *Political Argument*, Routledge and Kegan Paul, London.

—— (1973), *The Liberal Theory of Justice*, Clarendon Press, Oxford.

Becker, G. S. (1985), 'Public policies, pressure groups, and dead weight costs', *Journal of Public Economics*, 28: 329–47.

Blundell, R. W. (1988), 'Econometric issues in public economics', in P. G. Hare (ed.), *Surveys in Public Sector Economics*, Basil Blackwell, Oxford.

—— (1992), 'Labour supply and taxation: a survey', *Fiscal Studies*, 13 (Aug.): 15–40.

—— Meghir, C., Symons, E., and Walker, I. (1988), 'Labour supply specification and the empirical evaluation of tax reforms', *Journal of Public Economics*, 36: 23–52.

Boskin, M. J. (1972), 'The incidence of the payroll tax: an alternative approach', Stanford University Centre for Research in Economic Growth Memorandum 136.

—— (1975a), 'Efficiency aspects of the differential tax treatment of market and household economic activity', *Journal of Public Economics*, 4: 1–25.

—— (1975b), 'Notes on the tax treatment of human capital', National Bureau of Economic Research.

Bowles, S. (1985), 'The production process in a competitive economy:

Walrasian, Neo-Hobbesian and Marxian models', *American Economic Review*, 75: 16–36.

BREAK, G. F. (1974), 'The incidence and economic effects of taxation', in A. S. Blinder *et al.* (eds.), *The Economics of Public Finance*, Brookings Institution, Washington, DC.

BRENNAN, G. (1988), 'The public choice approach to tax reform', *Environment and Planning C: Government and Policy*, 6: 41–52.

—— and BUCHANAN, J. M. (1977), 'Towards a tax constitution for Leviathan', *Journal of Public Economics*, 8: 255–74.

—— —— (1978), 'Tax instruments as constraints on the disposition of public revenues', *Journal of Public Economics*, 9: 301–18.

BRITTAIN, J. A. (1972), *The Payroll Tax for Social Security*, Brookings Institution, Washington, DC.

BROWN, C. V. (1980), *Taxation and the Incentive to Work*, Oxford University Press, Oxford.

—— (1983), *Taxation and the Incentive to Work*, 2nd edn., Oxford University Press, Oxford.

—— and LEVIN, E. (1974), 'The effects of income taxation on overtime', *Economic Journal*, 84: 833–48.

BROWNING, E. K., and JOHNSON, W. R. (1984), 'The trade-off between equality and efficiency', *Journal of Political Economy*, 92: 175–203.

BUCHANAN, J. M. (1967), *Public Finance in Democratic Process*, University of North Carolina Press, Chapel Hill, NC.

—— (1984), 'The ethical limits of taxation', *Scandinavian Journal of Economics*, 86: 102–14.

—— and FAITH, R. L. (1987), 'Secession and the limits of taxation: toward a theory of internal exit', *American Economic Review*, 77: 1023–31.

—— and TULLOCK, G. (1962), *The Calculus of Consent*, University of Michigan Press, Ann Arbor, Mich.

BULOW, J. I., and SUMMERS, L. H. (1986), 'A theory of dual labor markets with application to industrial policy, discrimination, and Keynesian unemployment', *Journal of Labor Economics*, 4: 376–414.

BURTLESS, G. (1986), 'The work response to a guaranteed income: a survey of experimental evidence', in A. H. Munnell (ed.), *Lessons from the Income Maintenance Experiments*, Federal Reserve Bank of Boston, Conference Series No. 30.

—— and HAUSMAN, J. A. (1978), 'The effect of taxes on labor supply', *Journal of Political Economy*, 86: 1103–30.

—— and HAVEMAN, R. H. (1987a), 'Taxes and transfers: how much economic loss?', *Challenge* (Mar.–Apr.), 45–52.

—— —— (1987b), 'Taxes, transfers, and labor supply: the evolving views of U.S. economists', in *The Relevance of Public Finance for Policy-Making*, Wayne State University Press, Detroit.

Cain, G. G., and Watts, H. W. (1973) (eds.), *Income Maintenance and Labor Supply*, Rand McNally, Chicago.

Central Statistical Office (1987), *National Income and Expenditure*, HMSO, London.

Commission of the European Communities (1989), *Interim Report on a Specific Community Action Programme to Combat Poverty*, European Commission, Brussels.

Cukierman, A., and Meltzer, A. H. (1991), 'A political theory of progressive income taxation', in A. H. Meltzer, A. Cukierman, and S. F. Richard (eds.), *Political Economy*, Oxford University Press, Oxford.

Davidson, C., Martin, L., and Matusz, S. (1987), 'Search, unemployment, and the production of jobs', *Economic Journal*, 97: 857–76.

—— —— —— (1988), 'The structure of simple general equilibrium models with frictional unemployment', *Journal of Political Economy*, 96: 1267–93.

Deaton, A. (1983), 'An explicit solution to an optimal tax problem', *Journal of Public Economics*, 20: 333–46.

Department of Employment (1990), *New Earnings Survey 1990*, HMSO, London.

Dixit, A. K. (1976), 'Public finance in a Keynesian temporary equilibrium', *Journal of Economic Theory*, 12: 242–58.

—— and Sandmo, A. (1977), 'Some simplified formulae for optimal income taxation', *Scandinavian Journal of Economics*, 79: 417–23.

Doeringer, P. B., and Piore, M. J. (1971), *Internal Labor Markets and Manpower Analysis*, D. C. Heath, Lexington, Mass.

Duncan, A., and Jones, A. (1994), 'On the specification of labour supply models: a nonparametric evaluation', IFS Working Paper 94/3.

Feldstein, M. S. (1974), 'Tax incidence in a growing economy with variable factor supply', *Quarterly Journal of Economics*, 88: 551–73.

Foley, D. (1967), 'Resource allocation and the public sector', *Yale Economic Essays*, 7: 45–98.

Frey, B. S. (1976), 'Taxation in fiscal exchange: a comment', *Journal of Public Economics*, 6: 31–5.

Goodin, R. E. (1988), *Reasons for Welfare*, Princeton University Press, Princeton, NJ.

Griffin, J. (1986), *Well-Being*, Clarendon Press, Oxford.

Gronau, R. (1973), 'The effect of children on the housewife's value of time', *Journal of Political Economy*, 81 (Suppl.), S168–199.

Hall, R. E., and Rabushka, A. (1985), *The Flat Tax*, Hoover Institution Press, Stanford, Calif.

HARBERGER, A. C. (1962), 'The incidence of the corporation income tax', *Journal of Political Economy*, 70: 215–40.

HARRIS, J. R., and TODARO, M. (1970), 'Migration, unemployment, and development', *American Economic Review*, 60: 126–42.

HARSANYI, J. C. (1953), 'Cardinal utility in welfare economics and in the theory of risk-taking', *Journal of Political Economy*, 61: 434–5.

HAUSMAN, J. A. (1981), 'Labor supply', in H. J. Aaron and J. A. Pechman (eds.), *How Taxes Affect Economic Behavior*, Brookings Institution, Washington, DC.

—— (1983), 'Stochastic problems in the simulation of labor supply', in M. Feldstein (ed.), *Behavioral Simulation Methods in Tax Policy Analysis*, University of Chicago Press, Chicago.

—— (1985), 'The econometrics of nonlinear budget sets', *Econometrica*, 53: 1255–82.

—— and POTERBA, J. M. (1987), 'Household behavior and the Tax Reform Act of 1986', *Journal of Economic Perspectives* (Summer), 101–19.

HAYEK, F. A. (1960), *The Constitution of Liberty*, Routledge and Kegan Paul, London.

HECKMAN, J. J. (1974), 'Shadow prices, market wages and labor supply', *Econometrica*, 42: 1251–72.

—— (1983), Comment on J. A. Hausman, 'Stochastic problems in the simulation of labor supply', in M. Feldstein (ed.), *Behavioral Simulation Methods in Tax Policy Analysis*, University of Chicago Press, Chicago.

—— (1993), 'What has been learned about labor supply in the past twenty years?', *American Economic Review*, 83 (Papers and proceedings), 116–21.

HOCHMAN, H. M., and RODGERS, J. D. (1969), 'Pareto optimal redistribution', *American Economic Review*, 59: 542–57.

HOLMLUND, B., and LUNDBORG, P. (1989), 'Unemployment insurance schemes for reducing the natural rate of unemployment', *Journal of Public Economics*, 38: 1–15.

HURLEY, S. (1989), *Natural Reasons*, Oxford University Press, Oxford.

JOHNSON, H. G. (1971), *The Two-Sector Model of General Equilibrium*, Allen and Unwin, London.

JONES, R. W. (1965), 'The structure of simple general equilibrium models', *Journal of Political Economy*, 73: 557–72.

—— (1971), 'Distortions in factor markets and the general equilibrium model of production', *Journal of Political Economy*, 79: 437–59.

KENDALL, M. G., and STUART, A. (1969), *The Advanced Theory of Statistics*, vol. i, Griffin, London.

KESSELMAN, J. R. (1990), *Rate Structure and Personal Taxation*, Victoria University Press, Wellington.

KILLINGSWORTH, M. R. (1983), *Labor Supply*, Cambridge University Press, Cambridge.

KOTLIKOFF, L. J., and SUMMERS, L. H. (1987), 'Tax incidence', in A. J. Auerbach and M. S. Feldstein (eds.), *Handbook of Public Economics*, vol. ii, North-Holland, Amsterdam.

LINDAHL, E. (1928) 'Einige strittige Fragen der Steuertheorie', in H. Mayer (ed.), *Die Wirtschaftstheorie der Gegenwart*, iv, 282–304, trans. as 'Some controversial questions in the theory of taxation', in R. A. Musgrave and A. T. Peacock (eds.), *Classics in the Theory of Public Finance*, Macmillan, 1958: 214–32, page references to the English translation.

—— (1959), 'Om skatteprinciper och skattepolitik', in *Ekonomi Politik Samhälle*, Stockholm, trans. as 'Tax principles and tax policy', *International Economic Papers*, 10 (1960), 7–23, page references to the English translation.

LINDBECK, A. (1986), 'Limits to the welfare state', *Challenge* (Jan.–Feb.), 31–6.

—— (1988), 'Individual freedom and welfare state policy', *European Economic Review*, 32: 295–318.

—— and WEIBULL, J. W. (1993), 'A model of political equilibrium in a representative democracy', *Journal of Public Economics*, 51: 195–209.

MACURDY, T., GREEN, D., and PAARSCH, H. (1990), 'Assessing empirical approaches for analyzing taxes and labor supply', *Journal of Human Resources*, 25: 415–90.

McDONALD, I. M., and SOLOW, R. M. (1985), 'Wages and employment in a segmented labor market', *Quarterly Journal of Economics*, 100: 1115–41.

MACLEOD, W. B., and MALCOMSON, J. (1993), 'Wage premiums and profit maximisation in efficiency wage models', *European Economic Review*, 37: 1223–49.

McLURE, C. E. (1969), 'The inter-regional incidence of general regional taxes', *Public Finance*, 24: 457–84.

—— (1975), 'General equilibrium incidence analysis: the Harberger model after ten years', *Journal of Public Economics*, 4: 125–61.

MEADE, J. E. (1948), *Planning and the Price Mechanism*, Allen and Unwin, London.

—— (1972), 'Poverty in the Welfare State', *Oxford Economic Papers*, 24: 289–326.

MELTZER, A. H. (1991), 'Introduction' to A. H. Meltzer, A. Cukierman, and S. F. Richard (eds.), *Political Economy*, Oxford University Press, Oxford.

—— and RICHARD, S. F. (1981), 'A rational theory of the size of government', *Journal of Political Economy*, 89: 914–27.

—— —— (1985), 'A positive theory of in-kind transfers and the negative income tax', *Public Choice*, 47: 231–65.

MIESZKOWSKI, P. M. (1969), 'Tax incidence theory: the effects of taxes on the distribution of income', *Journal of Economic Literature*, 7: 1103–24.

MILL, J. S. (1843), *A System of Logic*, London.

MILLER, D. (1976), *Social Justice*, Clarendon Press, Oxford.

MIRRLEES, J. A. (1971), 'An exploration in the theory of optimum income taxation', *Review of Economic Studies*, 38: 175–208.

—— (1976), 'Optimal tax theory: a synthesis', *Journal of Public Economics*, 4: 27–33.

MROZ, T. (1987), 'The sensitivity of an empirical model of married women's hours of work to economic and statistical assumptions', *Econometrica*, 55: 765–99.

NOZICK, R. (1974), *Anarchy, State and Utopia*, Basil Blackwell, Oxford.

OKUN, A. M. (1975), *Equality and Efficiency*, Brookings Institution, Washington, DC.

OSWALD, A. (1986), 'Unemployment insurance and labour contracts under asymmetric information', *American Economic Review*, 76: 365–77.

—— and WALKER, I. (1993), 'Labour supply, contract theory and unions', IFS Working Paper 93/21.

PARKER, H. (1989), *Instead of the Dole*, Routledge, London.

—— (1993) (ed.), *Citizen's Income and Women*, BIRG Discussion Paper No. 2.

PECHMAN, J. A. (1971), *Federal Tax Policy*, 2nd edn., Brookings Institution, Washington, DC.

PENCAVEL, J. (1986), 'Labor supply of men: a survey', in O. Ashenfelter and R. Layard (eds.), *Handbook of Labor Economics*, vol. i, North-Holland, Amsterdam.

PUDNEY, S. (1989), *Modelling Individual Choice*, Basil Blackwell, Oxford.

—— and SUTHERLAND, H. (1994), 'How reliable are microsimulation results?', *Journal of Public Economics*, 53: 327–65.

RAWLS, J. (1971), *A Theory of Justice*, Harvard University Press, Cambridge, Mass.

RHYS WILLIAMS, J. (1943), *Something to Look Forward to*, MacDonald, London.

ROBERTS, K. W. S. (1977), 'Voting over income tax schedules', *Journal of Public Economics*, 8: 329–40.

ROSEN, H. S. (1980), 'What is labor supply and do taxes affect it?', *American Economic Review*, 70 (Papers and proceedings), 171–6.

SCHULTZ, T. W. (1961), 'Investment in human capital', *American Economic Review*, 51: 1–17.

SEADE, J. K. (1977), 'On the shape of optimal tax schedules', *Journal of Public Economics*, 7: 203–36.

SEN, A. K. (1970), 'The impossibility of a Paretian Liberal', *Journal of Political Economy*, 78: 152–7.

—— (1974), 'Informational bases of alternative welfare approaches', *Journal of Public Economics*, 3: 387–403.

—— (1985), 'Well-Being, agency and freedom: the Dewey Lectures 1984', *Journal of Philosophy*, 82: 169–221.

—— (1988), 'Freedom of choice: concept and content', *European Economic Review*, 32: 269–94.

—— and WILLIAMS, B. (1982) (eds.), *Utilitarianism and Beyond*, Cambridge University Press, Cambridge.

SHAPIRO, C., and STIGLITZ, J. E. (1984), 'Equilibrium unemployment as a worker discipline device', *American Economic Review*, 74: 433–44.

SLEMROD, J., YITZHAKI, S., MAYSHAR, J., and LUNDHOLM, M. (1994), 'The optimal two-bracket linear income tax', *Journal of Public Economics*, 53: 269–90.

STAFFORD, F. P. (1985), 'Income-maintenance policy and work effort: learning from experiments and labor market studies', in J. A. Hausman and D. A. Wise (eds.), *Social Experimentation*, University of Chicago Press, Chicago.

STERN, N. H. (1976), 'On the specification of optimum income taxation', *Journal of Public Economics*, 6: 123–62.

STIGLITZ, J. E. (1982), 'Alternative theories of wage determination and unemployment', in M. Gersovitz *et al.* (eds.), *The Theory and Experience of Economic Development*, Allen and Unwin, London.

—— (1988), *Economics of the Public Sector*, W. W. Norton, New York, 2nd edn.

TOWNSEND, P. B. (1979), *Poverty in the United Kingdom*, Allen Lane, London.

—— (1993), *The International Analysis of Poverty*, Harvester Wheatsheaf, Hemel Hempstead.

TUOMALA, M. (1990), *Optimal Income Tax and Redistribution*, Oxford University Press, Oxford.

VAN DE KLUNDERT, T. (1988), 'Wage differentials and employment in a two-sector model with a dual labour market', unpublished paper.

WALES, T. J., and WOODLAND, A. D. (1979), 'Labour supply and progressive taxes', *Review of Economic Studies*, 46: 83–95.

WEBB, S., and WEBB, B. (1911), *The Prevention of Destitution*, London.

WILLIAMS, B. (1981), *Moral Luck*, Cambridge University Press, Cambridge.

ZELLNER, A., and ROSSI, P. E. (1986), 'Evaluating the methodology of social experiments', in A. H. Munnell (ed.), *Lessons from the Income Maintenance Experiments*, Federal Reserve Bank of Boston, Conference Series No. 30.

Index

3 5282 00553 8429